YC

Travel guide

2025 and Beyond

Your Pioneering Handbook for an Extraordinary Urban Adventure with Expert Tips to Avoiding the Crowd

Cash Grey

Copyright © 2024 by Cash Grey

All rights reserved. No part of this publication may be reproduced, distributed, or transmitted in any form or by any means, including photocopying, recording, or other electronic or mechanical methods, without the prior written permission of the publisher, except in the case of brief quotations embodied in critical reviews and certain other noncommercial uses permitted by copyright law.

Table of contents

Table of contents   2
Introduction to York   5
    A Journey to Remember: My Unforgettable Adventure in York   5
Chapter 1: Welcome to York   9
    1.1 A Brief Overview of York's History   10
    1.2 Geography Overview   13
    1.3 Cultural Diversity   16
    1.4 York Today   21
Chapter 2: Planning Your Trip   29
    2.1 Selecting the Best Time to Visit   29
    2.2 Determining the Ideal Duration   32
    2.3 Entry Requirements and Visa Information   33
    2.4 Packing Essentials and What to Wear   36
Chapter 3: Transportations   45
    3.1 Getting to York   45
    3.2 Navigating Local Transportation   49
    3.3 Renting a Car   53
    3.4 Biking and Walking   57
Chapter 4: Exploring Historical Treasures   63
    4.1 The Shambles: A Medieval Marvel   63
    4.2 York Minster: Iconic Gothic Cathedral   65
    4.3 Clifford's Tower and York Castle   68
    4.4 Jorvik Viking Centre: Unveiling Viking History   71
    4.5 York City Walls: A Stroll through Time   73
    4.6 Treasurer's House and Its Ghostly Tales   76

Chapter 5: Cultural Delights 79
5.1 York's Thriving Arts and Music Scene 79
5.2 The Theatre Royal and Grand Opera House 81
5.3 York Art Gallery: A Collection of Artistic Gems 84
5.4 Festivals and Events Calendar 87
5.5 Exploring York's Literature Connections 91
5.6 Quaint Bookshops and Literary Sites 94

Chapter 6: Culinary Journey Through York 97
6.1 Traditional Yorkshire Pudding and Roast Dinner 97
6.2 The Famous Betty's Tea Room 100
6.3 Food Markets: Shambles Market, Newgate Market 103
6.4 Exploring York's Chocolate Heritage 106
6.5 International and Fusion Cuisine 108

Chapter 7: Nature and Relaxation 111
7.1 Rowntree Park: Serene Riverside Escape 111
7.2 York Museum Gardens: Where History Meets Nature 113
7.3 Boat Cruises on the River Ouse 116
7.4 Day Trips to the Yorkshire Dales 119
7.5 Biking and Hiking Trails 122
7.6 Relaxing Spas and Wellness Centers 125

Chapter 8: Hidden Gems and Local Secrets 129
8.1 York's Snickelways: Hidden Medieval Paths 129
8.2 York's Cat Trail: Feline-Inspired

Exploration	131
8.3 Ghost Walks and Haunted York	133
8.4 Homestead Park: A Local Favorite	136
8.5 Off-the-Beaten-Path Museums	139
8.6 Meeting Locals: Cultural Exchange	141
Chapter 9: Shopping and Souvenirs	**145**
9.1 Coney Street and High Petergate:	145
9.2 Unique Souvenirs from York	148
9.3 Practical Shopping Tips	152
Chapter 10: Nightlife and Entertainment	**155**
10.1 Late-Night Activities	155
10.2 Bars and Pubs	158
10.3 Nightclubs	160
Chapter 11: Accommodation Options	**163**
11.1 Luxury Hotels	163
11.2 Boutique and Mid-Range Hotels	164
11.3 Guesthouses and B&Bs	166
11.4 Self-Catering Apartments	167
11.5 Hostels and Budget Accommodation	169
11.6 Unique Stays	171
Chapter 12: Practical Information	**175**
12.1 Currency and Payment Options	175
12.2 Packing Essentials and What to Wear	178
12.3 Health and Safety	181
12.4 Local Laws and Customs	183
12.5 Avoiding Crowds	185
12.6 Day Trips	188
BONUS	**191**
An Excellent 3-Day Itinerary	191
Conclusion	**195**

Introduction to York

A Journey to Remember: My Unforgettable Adventure in York

Amidst the hustle and bustle of everyday life, there are moments that shimmer like hidden gems, waiting to be discovered. One such gem twinkled brightly during my recent trip to York—a city that effortlessly combines history, charm, and a touch of magic.

As I stepped onto the cobbled streets of York, the air carried a sense of anticipation. The towering spires of York Minster seemed to wink at me from afar, inviting me into a world where time itself felt like a plaything.

My journey began with a leisurely stroll through the Shambles—a labyrinth of crooked buildings that whispered secrets of centuries gone by. It was as if the spirits of medieval merchants still lingered, their laughter echoing through the narrow passageways. I couldn't help but smile as I imagined the stories these timeworn walls held.

The day's adventures led me to the York Cat Trail—an enchanting treasure hunt of feline sculptures that adorned the city's nooks and crannies. Each cat had its own personality, from a regal tabby lounging on a windowsill to a mischievous kitten peeking out from a flower pot. With my map in hand, I embarked on a playful quest, not only discovering the cats but also unraveling the city's secrets one pawprint at a time.

The soothing melody of a street musician's violin led me to the banks of the River Ouse. As I gazed at the water, a riverboat glided by, its passengers enraptured by tales of York's history. I realized that in this city, the past and present coexisted harmoniously, each brick and cobblestone weaving a tapestry of stories that echoed through time.

No trip to York would be complete without a visit to its bustling markets. The Shambles Market was a vibrant mosaic of colors and flavors, where local vendors shared their stories along with their wares. I indulged in a warm Yorkshire pudding, savoring its comforting embrace and feeling as though I had found the heart of Yorkshire's culinary soul.

As the sun dipped below the horizon, I found myself atop the city walls—a vantage point that offered a breathtaking panorama of York's splendor. The city's golden glow was a testament to its enduring allure, a place where the past danced with the present to create an unforgettable symphony.

As I bid farewell to York, I couldn't help but feel a sense of gratitude for the moments that had woven themselves into the tapestry of my journey. Each footstep had been a brushstroke on a canvas of memories, painting a picture that I would carry with me always.

And so, my trip to York became not just a journey through a city, but a voyage through time, an exploration of hidden corners and a heartwarming encounter with history. As I boarded my train, I couldn't help but smile, knowing that I had unearthed a treasure trove of experiences in a city that felt like home from the very first step.

Chapter 1: Welcome to York

Welcome to York, a city steeped in history, mystery, and the beauty of a bygone era. As you step into its cobblestone streets and beneath the shadows of its ancient walls, you're transported into a world where tales of kings, conquerors, and craftsmen intertwine to create a tapestry of captivating narratives.

With each footfall, you'll walk in the footsteps of Romans who laid the city's foundations, Vikings who left their mark on its culture, and medieval artisans who crafted its architectural wonders. York's rich past lives on in its timeworn buildings, narrow snickelways, and the echoes of history that seem to whisper from every corner.

But York isn't a city trapped in the past; it's a vibrant, evolving hub where history merges seamlessly with the present. Here, you'll find contemporary art galleries nestled beside medieval churches, bustling markets held within centuries-old marketplaces, and a delightful blend of traditional Yorkshire hospitality with a modern flair.

As you explore the city, you'll encounter the ethereal beauty of York Minster, the intrigue of winding lanes in The Shambles, and the charm of local shops and cafes that invite you to savor every moment. The River Ouse flows calmly, bearing witness to the stories etched into its banks, while the city walls stand as silent sentinels, guarding the secrets of generations.

In this guide, we'll be your compass, leading you through the alleys of history, the avenues of culture, and the pathways to hidden gems. Whether you're here for a short stay or an extended exploration, whether you seek the excitement of festivals or the solace of tranquil gardens, York has something extraordinary to offer.

1.1 A Brief Overview of York's History

A journey through York is a journey through time itself. This city's history is a tapestry woven with threads of triumph and turmoil, conquest and creation. From its humble origins to its pivotal role in shaping the nation, York's story unfolds across the ages.

Roman Foundations: Eboracum

The story of York begins nearly two thousand years ago when the Romans established the fortress of Eboracum in AD 71. This strategic outpost soon evolved into a bustling city, a testament to Roman engineering and governance. Eboracum witnessed the visit of Emperor Constantine and, later, the proclamation of his conversion to Christianity, which would leave a lasting impact on the city's cultural fabric.

Viking Saga: Jorvik

As the Roman Empire waned, York's fate took another turn with the arrival of the Vikings in the 9th century. Known as Jorvik in Old Norse, the Viking settlement left an indelible mark on the city's identity. The Jorvik Viking Centre today offers a vivid glimpse into the lives of its Norse inhabitants, their customs, and their tales of conquest and trade.

Norman Influence and the Wars of the Roses

The Norman Conquest in 1066 marked a new chapter in York's history. The construction of York Castle and the towering York Minster began, shaping the skyline and the spiritual essence of the city. York became a battleground during the Wars of the Roses, a conflict that pitted the Lancastrians against the Yorkists, earning York the title of "Kingmaker's City."

Turbulent Times and Renaissance

The following centuries were marked by moments of political unrest, religious changes, and economic shifts. York's medieval streets witnessed the rise and fall of monarchs, the enthusiasm of the Reformation, and the revival of trade. The city's Tudor and Stuart-era architecture, as well as its surviving guildhalls, stand as testaments to this period of evolution.

Industrial Revolution and Modern Era

The Industrial Revolution brought new prosperity and challenges to York. Its railways became pivotal in connecting the city to the wider world. The legacy of this era is seen in the preserved railway heritage and the National Railway Museum, which celebrates York's contribution to transportation history.

Present-day York: A Living Museum

Today, York is a living museum where the layers of its history coexist harmoniously with the present. The ancient city walls encircle the city's vibrant heart, protecting a wealth of stories within. Cobblestone streets lead to hidden snickelways, medieval churches, and modern markets. As you explore its winding paths, you'll feel the echoes of the past and the spirit of those who walked these streets before you.

The story of York continues to be written by its residents, its visitors, and the very stones upon which it stands. Every building, every landmark, and every whisper of the wind carries a piece of this city's remarkable history.

1.2 Geography Overview

York is located in the northern part of England, in the county of North Yorkshire. Its strategic geographical position has played a crucial role in its history and development, being a crossroads between the north and south of England and an important hub for trade, defense, and cultural exchange.

Location

York is situated approximately halfway between London and Edinburgh, making it an important connecting point in the heart of the United Kingdom. The city is located at the confluence of two rivers: the River Ouse and the River Foss. This riverside location provided significant advantages for trade and transport throughout its history, especially during the Roman and Viking periods.

Topography and Landscape

The topography of York is largely flat, with gentle undulations in the surrounding areas. The city is built on low-lying ground, which has made it prone to occasional flooding, particularly from the River Ouse. However, modern flood defenses have been implemented to mitigate this risk.

York is surrounded by rich, fertile farmland, with the Vale of York to the west. This fertile land has supported agriculture for centuries and contributed to the city's wealth, particularly during the medieval period.

Climate: Changing Seasons and English Temperance

York experiences a temperate maritime climate, typical of much of the United Kingdom. The climate is characterized by mild temperatures, moderate rainfall, and a fair amount of seasonal variation.

1. **Spring (March-May):** Spring in York brings a sense of renewal as the city's parks and gardens burst into bloom. Temperatures gradually rise during this period, ranging from around 7°C to 13°C (45°F to 55°F), making it a pleasant time to explore the city on foot.
2. **Summer (June - August):** York's summer months are relatively warm, with temperatures averaging between 14°C and 20°C (57°F to 68°F). This is a popular time for tourists to visit, enjoying the longer daylight hours and the city's outdoor attractions.
3. **Autumn (September - November):** As autumn arrives, the city's parks and trees transform into a riot of colors. Temperatures begin to cool down, ranging from around 8°C to 14°C (46°F to 57°F), and it's a wonderful time to explore York's cultural offerings.
4. **Winter (December - February):** York experiences cool and often chilly winters, with temperatures averaging around 2°C to 6°C (36°F to 43°F). While it's the quietest tourist season, the city's festive decorations and cozy ambiance make it an enchanting time for those who prefer cooler temperatures.

Rainfall and Sunshine:

York experiences moderate rainfall throughout the year, with slightly wetter months during the fall and winter. July tends to be the driest month, while October and November are often the wettest. The city enjoys around 1,500 to 1,700 hours of sunshine annually, ensuring a fair share of bright days to complement its historical charm.

Connectivity and Transport

York's central location makes it a key transportation hub in the UK. It is well connected by road, with the A1(M) motorway linking it to London in the south and Scotland to the north. The city's railway station is one of the busiest in the UK, serving as a major stop on the East Coast Main Line, with high-speed rail links to cities like London (around 2 hours away) and Edinburgh (2.5 hours).

In terms of air travel, York is close to major airports such as Leeds Bradford Airport (around 30 miles away) and Manchester Airport, both of which provide domestic and international flights.

Surrounding Areas

York sits within reach of several iconic natural landscapes. To the north, the rolling hills of the North York Moors National Park offer a scenic escape, while to the west, the Yorkshire Dales are known for their picturesque valleys and rugged terrain. The east coast of Yorkshire, with its cliffs and seaside towns such as Whitby and

Scarborough, is a short drive away, making York a perfect base for exploring the region's natural beauty.

In summary, York's geographical location has made it a crucial city throughout history, from its Roman roots to its development as a medieval powerhouse. Surrounded by rivers, fertile lands, and important natural landscapes, the city is both well-connected and endowed with natural resources that have contributed to its lasting prosperity.

1.3 Cultural Diversity

York, while often celebrated for its rich history and architectural wonders, is also a city that reflects an increasingly vibrant and diverse cultural mosaic. Over centuries, various peoples and traditions have contributed to the city's cultural identity, making York a fascinating blend of ancient heritage and modern multiculturalism.

Historical Influences on Culture

1. **Roman and Viking Legacy:** York's cultural diversity can be traced back to its foundations as the Roman city of Eboracum, established in AD 71. The city became a Roman provincial capital, attracting people from across the Roman Empire. Soldiers, traders, and officials from various regions, including Europe, Africa, and the Middle East, mingled in York's streets,

contributing to a mix of influences in everything from architecture to customs.

In the 9th century, York became a Viking hub known as Jorvik, under Scandinavian rule. This era introduced Nordic cultural elements, with influences on local governance, trade, and even language, some of which persist today. The city's renowned Jorvik Viking Centre keeps this heritage alive, drawing attention to the blend of cultures in early York.

2. **Medieval Multiculturalism:** By the medieval period, York was a major center of religion, trade, and education. It attracted merchants and clergy from across Europe, particularly from Flanders, Germany, and France. Jewish communities played a significant role during the medieval period, establishing a rich cultural presence before their expulsion in the 13th century. Today, the Clifford's Tower site memorializes the tragic massacre of Jews in 1190, serving as a reminder of the long-standing historical ties of Jewish communities to the city.

Modern-Day Cultural Diversity

1. **Immigration and Communities:** In recent decades, York has become more multicultural, with waves of immigration from various parts of the world. The city has seen the arrival of people from South Asia, Africa, Eastern Europe, and the Caribbean, who have brought their cultural, religious, and culinary traditions with them.
   - South Asian Communities: The city has a growing South Asian population, particularly from India, Pakistan, and Bangladesh. This has enriched York's cultural and culinary landscape, with Indian and Pakistani restaurants, grocery stores, and cultural festivals becoming a common feature of the city.
   - Eastern European Influence: In the wake of EU expansion in the 2000s, there was an influx of immigrants from Poland, Romania, and other Eastern European countries. These communities have contributed to the workforce, particularly in service industries, construction, and agriculture, while also introducing their languages, traditions, and foods to York's cultural tapestry.
2. **Religion and Worship:** York is home to a variety of religious communities, reflecting its growing diversity. While York Minster, the grand Gothic cathedral, remains an iconic symbol of Christianity in the city, places of worship for other religions are now a visible part of the community.

- **Islam:** The city has a small but growing Muslim population. The York Mosque and Islamic Centre serves the local Muslim community and engages in interfaith dialogues and cultural exchange activities, promoting a harmonious relationship between different faiths.
- **Judaism:** Though York's Jewish community faced persecution in the medieval era, it has seen a resurgence in modern times. York's small Jewish community is active in preserving Jewish heritage and fostering education and understanding about Jewish history.
- **Other Faiths:** In addition to Christianity and Islam, there are also smaller communities of Buddhists, Hindus, Sikhs, and people of other faiths, reflecting the multicultural fabric of the city.

3. **Festivals and Celebrations:** York celebrates its diversity through various cultural festivals and events, which attract both locals and tourists alike. These festivals not only honor the city's historical roots but also showcase its modern multicultural influences.
   - **Yorkshire Festival of Diversity:** A vibrant celebration of the cultures and traditions that make up York's community today, featuring food stalls, music, dance performances, and exhibitions representing global cultures.

- **Ebor Festival and Other Historical Events:** While historical in nature, these festivals often incorporate modern elements of multiculturalism, inviting performers and participants from diverse backgrounds to celebrate York's shared heritage.
- **Food Festivals:** York's food scene has flourished thanks to its cultural diversity. Events like the York Food and Drink Festival often include international cuisines, from Indian curries to Polish pierogi and Mediterranean mezze, reflecting the multicultural tastes of York's residents and visitors.

4. **Arts and Education:** York is home to two universities—The University of York and York St John University—which have drawn students and academics from around the world. This influx of international students has further diversified the city, introducing new perspectives and fostering cross-cultural exchanges.

The art scene in York has also been influenced by its cultural diversity. Galleries, theatres, and music venues showcase not only British talent but also artists and performers from various cultures. This has given rise to new and exciting collaborations, where traditional British arts blend with global influences.

Cultural Integration and Challenges

As with many cities experiencing demographic change, York has had to navigate challenges related to integration and ensuring that all communities feel welcome and included. Efforts by local councils, community organizations, and educational institutions have focused on promoting inclusivity, celebrating diversity, and addressing any tensions that arise from cultural differences.

York's rich historical background as a city that has always embraced people from different regions has helped in fostering a spirit of tolerance and understanding. Cultural diversity in York is a testament to its long-standing tradition of openness, resilience, and adaptability.

York is not just a city where history comes alive but also a modern, vibrant community that continues to evolve. Its cultural diversity adds a dynamic layer to the city's heritage, making it a truly global city that honors both its past and its future.

1.4 York Today

In the present day, York is a thriving, dynamic city that skillfully balances its rich historical heritage with the demands of modern life. Known for its medieval streets, iconic landmarks, and cultural significance, the city has also evolved into a hub for education, tourism, technology, and the arts. With its growing diversity, modern amenities, and strong connection to its past, York offers a unique blend of tradition and progress.

Population and Demographics

Today, York is home to approximately 210,000 residents, with a population that is growing steadily. While historically the city's demographics were more homogeneous, York has become increasingly diverse in recent decades. A mix of long-time residents, international students, and immigrants from different parts of the world has transformed the city into a more multicultural community.

York's demographic profile includes a large number of students, thanks to the two prominent universities: The University of York and York St John University. These institutions have drawn students and faculty from across the globe, adding youthful energy and a global outlook to the city's identity.

Economy

Once an important medieval center for trade and craftsmanship, York's economy today is driven by a mix of industries. The city's heritage of innovation and trade continues, but now with a modern twist.

1. **Tourism:** Tourism remains one of York's most significant economic drivers. Millions of visitors come to York each year, drawn by its famous landmarks like York Minster, The Shambles, and Jorvik Viking Centre. The city's charm lies in its ability to cater to history buffs, families, and travelers seeking a cultural getaway. In response to this, hospitality, accommodation, and retail have flourished, supporting thousands of jobs and contributing significantly to the local economy.
2. **Technology and Innovation:** In recent years, York has emerged as a center for digital and creative industries, making it one of the UK's fastest-growing tech hubs. The city's proximity to major urban centers like Leeds and Manchester, combined with its high quality of life, has attracted technology startups and digital agencies. The Guildhall and York Science Park are just a few examples of innovation spaces fostering new talent and business development in the region.
3. **Education and Research:** York is also a center for education and research, with The University of York being one of the top institutions in the country. It contributes significantly to local employment and the economy. The university's research output, particularly in areas such as biology, chemistry, and social sciences, has positioned York as a city known for academic excellence and innovation.

4. **Traditional Industries:** While York has diversified its economy, some of its traditional industries still play an important role. The food and drink sector, for instance, has deep roots in the city's history, particularly with York's famous chocolate-making legacy. Companies such as Nestlé and Terry's have been long-standing names in the region, and while large-scale production has shifted, smaller artisanal food producers have helped maintain this tradition.

Urban Development and Infrastructure

York is a city that balances the preservation of its historic core with modern urban development. In recent years, the city has seen significant investment in infrastructure to cater to its growing population and tourism needs.

1. **Transportation:** York's central location in the UK makes it an important transportation hub. The city's railway station is one of the busiest outside London, providing easy access to major cities across the country. In addition, York is known for its cycling-friendly infrastructure, and many residents opt to navigate the city on bikes, particularly in the city center, where traffic restrictions encourage pedestrian and cyclist movement. Efforts to improve public transport services, including electric buses and sustainable travel initiatives, reflect the city's

commitment to reducing its carbon footprint and enhancing urban mobility.
2. **Housing and Urban Expansion:** York's growing population has led to the expansion of housing projects on the outskirts of the city. New developments aim to cater to both the local population and newcomers, with a focus on sustainable and eco-friendly housing. However, as with many historic cities, maintaining the balance between modern development and preserving York's unique character is a challenge. The city continues to carefully manage its growth to avoid overwhelming its historic center.
3. **Sustainability Initiatives:** As part of York's commitment to becoming a greener city, sustainability initiatives have been implemented across various sectors. The city council has set ambitious goals for reducing carbon emissions, with investments in green spaces, renewable energy, and waste management. The historic city walls and public parks, such as York Museum Gardens and Rowntree Park, offer residents and visitors access to well-maintained green spaces that promote environmental awareness and well-being.

Culture and Lifestyle

York's cultural scene is vibrant, offering a range of experiences that blend its historical legacy with contemporary influences.

1. **Arts and Entertainment:** The city has a thriving arts community, with numerous galleries, theatres, and music venues. York Theatre Royal, one of the UK's oldest theatres, continues to host acclaimed performances, while the Grand Opera House stages everything from musicals to comedy shows. For visual arts enthusiasts, the York Art Gallery features an eclectic mix of classic and modern art.
2. **Food and Drink:** The culinary scene in York has also diversified, with a growing number of restaurants offering global cuisine alongside traditional British fare. The city is known for its food markets, such as Shambles Market, where local produce and street food stalls create a lively atmosphere. The rise of artisanal food producers and independent cafés reflects the city's love for quality food, and York's reputation as a destination for food lovers continues to grow.
3. **Events and Festivals:** York's cultural calendar is packed with events and festivals throughout the year. Some of the city's most popular events include:
   - **The York Food and Drink Festival:** A celebration of local produce and global cuisine.

- **Yorkshire Day:** Held every August, this event showcases the best of Yorkshire's culture and traditions.
- **York Literature Festival:** Bringing together authors, poets, and book lovers from around the world.

4. **Education and Learning:** In addition to its universities, York has excellent primary and secondary schools, making it an attractive destination for families. The city's libraries, museums, and historical sites also offer abundant learning opportunities for both residents and tourists, enriching the cultural and intellectual life of the community.

A City for the Future

York's success lies in its ability to honor its past while embracing the future. With its commitment to sustainability, diversity, and technological innovation, the city is poised to continue thriving as a vibrant, modern destination that never loses sight of its historical roots. Whether as a place to live, work, study, or visit, York today offers an unparalleled experience that merges old-world charm with the conveniences of contemporary life.

Chapter 2: Planning Your Trip

2.1 Selecting the Best Time to Visit

Selecting the best time to visit York depends on a combination of factors, including your preferences, interests, and the type of experience you're seeking. Here is a guide to assist you in making a knowledgeable choice:

1. **Weather and Climate:** Consider the type of weather you prefer. If you enjoy milder temperatures and blooming gardens, spring (March-May) might be appealing. If you prefer

warm weather and longer daylight hours for outdoor activities, summer (June - August) is a great choice. Autumn (September - November) offers colorful foliage, and winter (December - February) brings a cozy, festive atmosphere.

2. **Crowds and Tourist Season:** If you prefer a quieter experience with fewer crowds, aim for the shoulder seasons of spring and autumn. These periods offer pleasant weather without the peak tourist influx of summer. Winter can also be quieter, except during the holiday season when festive events attract visitors.
3. **Festivals and Events:** Check the event calendar for festivals or events that align with your interests. York hosts various events throughout the year, such as the Jorvik Viking Festival in February, the York Food and Drink Festival in September, and Christmas markets in December.
4. **Historical Sites and Attractions:** Consider the operating hours of historical sites, museums, and attractions you want to visit. Some attractions might have limited hours or closures during the off-peak months, so plan accordingly.
5. **Budget:** Travel costs can vary depending on the season. Accommodation, transportation, and even entrance fees to attractions might be higher during peak tourist season. Traveling during shoulder or off-peak seasons could offer cost savings.

6. **Seasonal Experiences:** Think about the experiences you want to have. Do you want to see York's gardens in full bloom during spring? Are you interested in outdoor activities in the summer? Do you love the charm of holiday markets in winter? Your interests can help guide your timing.
7. **Personal Preference:** Ultimately, the best time to visit York is the time that aligns with your preferences. Think about the kind of travel experience you enjoy – whether it's a bustling atmosphere, serene exploration, festive celebrations, or a specific weather type.
8. **Flexibility:** If possible, consider planning your trip with some flexibility. Weather can be unpredictable, and unexpected opportunities might arise during your visit. Being open to adjusting your plans can enhance your experience.

Ultimately, the best time to visit York depends on what you value most in your travel experience. Whether you're drawn to historical sites, cultural events, seasonal beauty, or a combination of these factors, York offers a range of experiences throughout the year.

2.2 Determining the Ideal Duration

Determining the ideal duration for your visit to York depends on the depth of experience you seek, your interests, and the pace at which you like to travel. Here are some factors to consider when deciding how many days to spend in York:

1. **Must-See Attractions:** Make a list of the key attractions and sites you want to visit in York. Some, like York Minster and the Shambles, can be explored in a few hours, while others, like museums and historical sites, might require more time. Calculate the time you'd like to allocate for these must-see places.
2. **Exploration and Relaxation:** Consider how much time you'd like to dedicate to leisurely exploration, whether it's strolling along the city walls, exploring parks, or enjoying local cafes. York's ambiance is best experienced when you have time to take in its surroundings at a comfortable pace.
3. **Special Interests:** If you have specific interests such as history, art, or culinary experiences, factor in additional time for visiting related museums, and galleries, and trying out local cuisines.
4. **Day Trips:** York's central location makes it a great base for day trips to nearby attractions such as Castle Howard, the Yorkshire Dales, or

Whitby. If you plan to explore these areas, allocate extra days for day trips.
5. **Events and Festivals:** Check if are any special events or festivals happening during your visit that you'd like to participate in. These might require additional time in your itinerary.
6. **Relaxation vs. Activity:** Consider your preferred balance between active sightseeing and leisure time. Some travelers enjoy a packed itinerary, while others prefer a more relaxed pace.
7. **Unplanned Moments:** Leave some room in your itinerary for unplanned moments – a charming street you stumble upon, conversations with locals, or serendipitous discoveries that can enrich your experience.
8. **Travel Style:** Think about your travel style. Are you someone who likes to immerse deeply in a few places, or do you prefer covering more ground in a shorter time?

2.3 Entry Requirements and Visa Information

Entry Requirements

- **Passport:** All visitors to the United Kingdom, including York, must have a valid passport. Make sure your passport is valid for at least six months after the day you intend to depart.

- **Visa Requirement:** Visa requirements depend on your nationality and the purpose and duration of your visit. Citizens of the European Union (EU) and European Economic Area (EEA) countries do not typically need a visa for short visits (tourism, business meetings, etc.) but should check for any specific requirements due to Brexit changes. Non-EU/EEA citizens will likely need a visa for entry, depending on their nationality and the purpose of their visit.
- **Electronic Travel Authorization (ETA):** The UK has introduced a new system called the Electronic Travel Authorization (ETA) for visitors from visa-exempt countries. This system requires travelers to obtain an ETA online before traveling to the UK. The ETA is not a visa but a mandatory pre-travel authorization.
- **Immigration Form:** Upon arrival in the UK, you might be required to fill out an immigration form. Ensure that the information you submit is accurate and comprehensive.

Visa Information

- **Tourist Visa:** If you're planning a short visit to York for tourism purposes, you'll typically enter under the "Standard Visitor Visa" category. This visa allows you to stay in the UK for up to six months for tourism, visiting

family or friends, or participating in short courses.
- **Work or Study Visa:** If you plan to work, study, or engage in any form of employment or business activities in the UK, you will likely need to apply for a specific visa, such as the Tier 2 (General) visa for work or a Student visa for studying.
- **Visa Application Process:** To apply for a visa, you'll usually need to complete an online application form, pay the required fees, and provide necessary documents such as proof of accommodation, financial capability, and purpose of visit. Processing times and requirements can vary, so it's essential to start the application process well in advance of your planned travel dates.

Resources for Current Information

For the most accurate and up-to-date information about entry requirements and visa regulations for visiting York, the UK government's official website and the website of the British Embassy or Consulate in your country are reliable sources. You can also consult with your local UK embassy or consulate for guidance on visa application procedures specific to your nationality and circumstances.

Keep in mind that immigration policies can change, so it's crucial to double-check the requirements closer to your travel dates to ensure a smooth entry into the United Kingdom and your visit to York.

2.4 Packing Essentials and What to Wear

When planning a trip to York, it's important to consider the city's climate, activities, and style of sightseeing. Given the weather variability in the UK and the mix of urban exploration and historical attractions, being prepared with the right clothing and essentials will help you enjoy your visit to the fullest.

Packing Essentials for York

1. **Travel Documents:**
   - **Passport and Visa (if applicable):** Ensure you have valid travel documents. While York is in the UK, non-UK visitors will need to bring identification and any required travel visas.
   - **Accommodation Confirmations:** Printed or digital versions of your hotel or Airbnb reservations.
   - **Transportation Tickets:** Have printed or digital copies of train, bus, or flight tickets if necessary.
   - **Travel Insurance:** Always a good idea to have, especially for international travelers.
2. **Weather-Appropriate Clothing:**

- Waterproof Jacket or Raincoat: York, like much of the UK, experiences frequent rainfall, especially in the autumn and winter months. A lightweight, waterproof jacket will be invaluable for keeping dry while exploring the city.
- Comfortable Walking Shoes: The city is best explored on foot, especially with its cobblestone streets and historic areas. Sturdy, comfortable shoes are essential, especially if you plan on walking along the city walls or taking guided tours. Waterproof shoes are a plus in case of rain.
- Layers: York's weather can be unpredictable, so packing layers is key. Thin sweaters, cardigans, or light jackets are perfect for layering on cooler days or in the evening.
- Umbrella: While not essential, a compact travel umbrella is useful to carry, especially during the rainy months.

3. **Day-to-Day Essentials:**
   - **Backpack or Crossbody Bag:** A small, comfortable bag for carrying your daily essentials while sightseeing. Make sure it has a secure zipper to protect your belongings in busy areas.
   - **Portable Charger:** Keeping your phone charged is important, especially if you're using it for maps, tickets, or taking photos.

- **Reusable Water Bottle:** Staying hydrated is important while walking around, and many attractions in York have water refill stations.
- **Sunscreen:** Even on cloudy days, UV rays can be strong. Sunscreen is essential, particularly if you plan to be outside for long periods.
- **Sunglasses:** For sunnier days, sunglasses will help protect your eyes and make outdoor exploration more comfortable.

4. **Electronics and Accessories:**
   - **Camera or Smartphone:** York is filled with photo-worthy spots, from York Minster to The Shambles. Make sure you have a camera or a smartphone with ample storage.
   - **UK Power Adapter (if coming from abroad):** The UK uses a three-pronged plug (Type G), so if you're coming from outside the UK, you'll need an adapter for your electronics.
5. **Guidebook or Map:** While digital maps are useful, a physical map or guidebook can be a handy backup, especially if you don't have consistent mobile service. You can also use it for planning your itinerary and noting places of interest.

What to Wear in York (By Season)

1. **Spring (March – May):** Temperatures in spring range from 8°C to 15°C (46°F to 59°F). It can be chilly in the mornings and evenings, but mild during the day.

What to Wear:

- Lightweight layers, such as long-sleeved shirts, cardigans, or light sweaters.
- A medium-weight jacket, preferably waterproof.
- Comfortable, closed-toe shoes or waterproof boots for walking.
- Scarves or hats for added warmth on cooler days.

Tips: Spring can be a bit rainy, so carry an umbrella or pack a raincoat. Pack brighter, transitional clothing as the weather warms up toward late spring.

2. **Summer (June – August):** Summer temperatures range from 13°C to 22°C (55°F to 72°F). While generally warm, occasional cool breezes and rain showers are common.

What to Wear:

- Light, breathable clothing like cotton T-shirts, blouses, and light dresses.
- A light jacket or sweater for cooler evenings.

- Comfortable sandals or walking shoes (opt for closed-toe if rain is forecasted).
- Sunglasses, hats, and sunscreen for sun protection.

Tips: Even in summer, it's wise to bring a light rain jacket or umbrella. Summer days in York can feel warm, but the temperature can drop in the evenings.

3. **Autumn (September – November):** Autumn is cool and often rainy, with temperatures ranging from 8°C to 15°C (46°F to 59°F).

What to Wear:

- Layers, including long-sleeved shirts, sweaters, and a warm coat.
- Waterproof boots or shoes, especially in October and November.
- Scarves, gloves, and hats as it can get quite chilly later in the season.

Tips: Autumn is one of the rainiest times of the year, so a sturdy umbrella and waterproof clothing are essentials. This season is also great for enjoying the fall colors in York's parks.

4. **Winter (December – February):** Winter in York can be cold, with temperatures ranging from 0°C to 7°C (32°F to 45°F). Snow is possible, but rain and wind are more common.

What to Wear:

- Warm clothing, including thermal layers, thick sweaters, and winter coats.
- Waterproof boots or sturdy shoes with good traction for wet or icy conditions.
- Gloves, scarves, and hats to keep warm, especially on windy days.
- A heavy-duty waterproof coat or insulated jacket.

Tips: Winters in York can feel damp and cold, so layering is essential. Having a warm and waterproof outer layer will keep you comfortable during outdoor sightseeing.

Specialty Items to Consider

- **Binoculars:** If you're interested in birdwatching or taking in the views from atop York Minster or the city walls, binoculars could enhance the experience.
- **Evening Attire:** York has a range of dining options, including upscale restaurants. If you plan to dine somewhere formal, pack a smarter outfit, such as a dress or a nice shirt and trousers.

Final Tips for Packing

- Check the weather forecast before your trip to pack accordingly, as York's weather can change quickly.

- If you're planning to visit attractions like York Minster, it's respectful to dress modestly (especially in places of worship).
- Bring extra memory cards or storage for your camera or phone, as York offers many photo opportunities.

Getting to York is relatively straightforward due to its central location and well-connected transportation network. Whether you're arriving by air, train, bus, or car, there are various options to suit your preferences. Here's an overview of how to get to York:

1. **By Air:**
    - **Leeds Bradford Airport (LBA):** This is the nearest international airport to York, located about 50 miles away. You can take a train, bus, or taxi from the airport to York.
    - **Manchester Airport (MAN):** While a bit farther (about 100 miles), Manchester Airport offers more international flight options. You can take a direct train from Manchester Airport to York, which takes around 2 hours.
    - **London Airports:** If you're flying into one of London's major airports (Heathrow,

Gatwick, Stansted, or Luton), you can take a direct train from London to York. The journey takes around 2-2.5 hours from London Kings Cross station.
2. **By Train:** York is well-connected by train services:
   - **London:** The East Coast Main Line connects York with London Kings Cross station. The journey takes around 2-2.5 hours.
   - **Other Cities:** Direct train services connect York with major cities like Edinburgh, Manchester, Liverpool, and Birmingham.
3. **By Bus:** There are local and interstate bus services that travel to and from York.
   - **National Express and Megabus:** These long-distance coach services connect York with various cities and towns across the UK.
4. **By Car:** If you prefer to drive, York is accessible by major roads:
   - **M1 and A1(M):** The M1 and A1(M) motorways connect York to the south and London.
   - **A19 and A59:** These roads link York to other cities and towns in the north and northeast.

Chapter 3: Transportations

3.1 Getting to York

York is a well-connected city, offering a variety of transportation options for visitors traveling from across the UK and internationally. Due to its central location, York is easily accessible by train, car, bus, or air, making it a convenient and popular destination for tourists.

By Train

York's railway station is one of the busiest and best-connected in the UK, offering fast and frequent services from major cities:

- **From London:** Trains operated by LNER (London North Eastern Railway) run frequently from London King's Cross to York, with a travel time of just under 2 hours. This is one of the fastest and most popular ways to reach York from the capital.
- **From Edinburgh:** York is about 2.5 hours away by train from Edinburgh Waverley station, also operated by LNER.
- **From Manchester:** Trains from Manchester Piccadilly to York take approximately 1.5 hours, making it a convenient option for those arriving into Manchester Airport.

- **From Leeds:** Local services from Leeds to York take about 25 minutes, making it a quick regional connection.

York Railway Station is located just outside the historic city walls and within walking distance of many key attractions, including York Minster and The Shambles.

By Air

While York does not have its own airport, it is easily accessible from several major airports in the region:

- **Leeds Bradford Airport (LBA):** The nearest airport to York, Leeds Bradford is about 30 miles (48 km) away. You can take a bus or taxi from the airport to Leeds Railway Station, where regular trains run to York in about 25 minutes. The total travel time is roughly 1-1.5 hours.
- **Manchester Airport (MAN):** Located about 80 miles (129 km) from York, Manchester Airport is another good option, especially for international travelers. There are direct train services from the airport to York, which take about 1.5-2 hours.
- **London Heathrow and London Gatwick Airports:** For those flying into London, take the Heathrow Express or Gatwick Express into central London and transfer to London King's Cross for a direct train to York (around 2 hours).

By Car

York is well connected by road, although driving into the city center can be challenging due to narrow streets and limited parking. However, it's an ideal option for those looking to explore the surrounding Yorkshire countryside or nearby towns.

- **From London:** The drive from London to York takes about 4-5 hours via the M1 and A1(M) motorways.
- **From Edinburgh:** Driving from Edinburgh takes around 4 hours via the A1 motorway.
- **From Manchester:** The journey from Manchester to York by car takes about 1.5-2 hours via the M62.

York offers several Park and Ride facilities around the city, where you can park your car and take a bus into the city center to avoid parking issues.

By Bus or Coach

For budget travelers, long-distance buses and coaches are an affordable option:

National Express and Megabus offer coach services from various UK cities to York. The travel time from London is typically around 5-6 hours, and from Manchester it is around 2-3 hours. The York Bus Station is centrally located, making it easy to access the city center once you arrive.

By Ferry (for International Travelers)

For travelers coming from mainland Europe, taking a ferry to the UK and then traveling to York by road or train can be an option. Ferries arrive at ports such as Hull (about 1 hour by car from York) or Newcastle (about 2 hours by car or train).

Transportation Tips

- **Advance Booking:** Train tickets in the UK can be expensive if purchased last minute. It's advisable to book in advance to secure the best prices, especially on LNER services.
- **Railcards:** If you're traveling by train frequently, consider getting a UK Railcard (e.g., 16-25 Railcard, Senior Railcard, or Two Together Railcard) for discounted fares.
- **Park and Ride:** If driving to York, use the Park and Ride services to avoid the hassle of parking in the city center. It's cost-effective and buses run frequently into town.

Whether you're traveling by train, car, or plane, York is easily accessible and well-connected, making it a convenient base for exploring both the city and the surrounding region of Yorkshire.

3.2 Navigating Local Transportation

York's local transportation system is designed to be efficient, convenient, and user-friendly, making it easy for visitors to explore the city and its surroundings. Here's a comprehensive guide on how to navigate local transportation in York, including buses, taxis, cycling, and walking.

Buses

Buses are a primary mode of transportation in York, offering extensive coverage throughout the city and nearby areas.

1. **Local Bus Services:** Operated by First York, the local buses connect various neighborhoods, shopping districts, and attractions. Key routes run frequently, especially between the city center and suburbs, ensuring easy access to places like York Designer Outlet and Rowntree Park.
2. **Park and Ride Services:** York has several Park and Ride facilities located on the outskirts of the city. This service allows you to park your car and take a bus into the city center, avoiding traffic and parking difficulties. Park and Ride locations include:
    - Rawcliffe Bar: North of the city
    - Designer Outlet: Near the shopping outlet
    - Askham Bar: South of the city

- Monks Cross: East of the city

Buses from these sites run every 10-15 minutes, making it a convenient option for travelers.

3. **Fares and Tickets:** You can purchase single, return, or day tickets on the bus or via the First Bus App. Day tickets are particularly cost-effective for those planning multiple journeys in a single day, as they allow unlimited travel on First York services. Consider the York Pass if you plan to visit many attractions, as it may include discounts on bus fares.

Taxis

Taxis are a reliable and convenient way to get around York, especially for late-night travel or when carrying luggage.

1. **Taxi Ranks:** Taxis are available at various ranks around the city, including at York Railway Station, Clifford Street, and St. Saviourgate.
2. **Booking a Taxi:** You can hail a taxi on the street or book one in advance through local taxi companies like York Taxis or Alpha Taxis.
3. **Ride-Sharing Services:** Uber operates in York, providing an app-based option for getting around the city conveniently.

Cycling

York is a bike-friendly city with many designated cycling paths and routes.

1. **Bike Rentals:** Several shops offer bike rentals, including Cycle Heaven, which provides options for daily or longer-term rentals. The city also has bike-sharing schemes, where you can hire bikes for short trips.
2. **Cycling Routes:** York has numerous dedicated bike lanes and scenic routes, including paths along the River Ouse and through parks. The Solar System Cycle Route is a popular choice for cyclists, offering an educational experience with scale models of the planets along the way.

Walking

Walking is one of the best ways to explore York, given its compact size and rich history.

1. **Pedestrian-Friendly City:** Many attractions, including York Minster, The Shambles, and Clifford's Tower, are within easy walking distance of each other. The city's pedestrianized areas and historic streets make for a pleasant walking experience.
2. **City Walls:** Consider walking along the City Walls, which offer a unique perspective of the city and its landmarks.

River Transport

Another charming way to experience York is through its waterways.

1. **Boat Tours:** Companies like City Cruises York offer sightseeing boat tours along the River Ouse, providing scenic views of the city's architecture and attractions.
2. You can also rent self-drive boats for a more personalized experience.

Accessibility

York is committed to making local transportation accessible to everyone:

1. **Buses:** Most local buses are equipped with ramps and designated spaces for wheelchairs.
2. **Taxi Services:** Many taxi companies in York offer accessible vehicles for those with mobility challenges.
3. **City Center:** The city center is generally accessible, although some cobbled streets may pose challenges for wheelchairs or strollers.

Navigating Tips

1. **Maps and Apps:** Use the First Bus App for real-time bus schedules and ticket purchases. Google Maps or Citymapper can help you navigate walking routes and public transportation options.

2. **Plan Ahead:** Check the bus schedules and routes ahead of time, especially during weekends or holidays, when services may vary.
3. **Stay Aware of Traffic:** While York is pedestrian-friendly, be mindful of cyclists and other pedestrians, especially in busy areas.

By utilizing York's local transportation options effectively, you can easily explore the city's rich history, culture, and attractions at your own pace. Whether you prefer walking along the historic streets, cycling through scenic paths, or hopping on a bus, York offers a convenient and enjoyable experience for all visitors.

3.3 Renting a Car

Renting a car can be a convenient option for exploring York and its beautiful surrounding areas. Whether you're planning to visit the picturesque Yorkshire Dales, the North York Moors, or nearby historic towns, having a car gives you the flexibility to travel at your own pace. Here's what you need to know about renting a car in York.

Choosing a Rental Company

Several well-known car rental companies operate in York, providing a range of vehicle options to suit different needs:

1. **National Companies:** Major brands like Hertz, Avis, Enterprise, Europcar, and Budget

have offices in York, often at the railway station or nearby.
2. **Local Companies:** Consider local rental services for competitive rates and personalized service. Companies like York Car Hire may offer attractive packages.

Tips for Choosing a Rental Company

- Compare prices and terms on platforms like Kayak, Rentalcars.com, or Expedia.
- Check customer reviews and ratings for reliability and customer service.

Booking a Car

1. **Advance Reservations:** It's advisable to book your car in advance, especially during peak tourist seasons. This not only ensures availability but often secures better rates.
2. **Pick-Up Locations:** You can choose to pick up your car at the airport, railway station, or city center locations, depending on your travel plans.

Rental Requirements

To rent a car in the UK, you typically need to meet the following requirements:

1. **Age:** Most companies require drivers to be at least 21 years old. Drivers under 25 may incur a young driver surcharge.

2. **Driver's License:** A valid driving license is necessary. If your license is not in English, you may need an International Driving Permit (IDP).
3. **Credit Card:** A credit card in the name of the main driver is usually required for the security deposit.
4. **Insurance:** Basic insurance is included, but you may want to consider additional coverage for peace of mind.

Understanding Rental Terms

1. **Mileage Limit:** Some rentals may have mileage limits, while others offer unlimited mileage. Be sure to check this detail.
2. **Fuel Policy:** Understand the fuel policy (e.g., full-to-full), meaning you pick up the car with a full tank and return it full to avoid extra charges.
3. **Additional Drivers:** If someone else will be driving, check the policy on adding additional drivers and any associated fees.

Driving in York

1. **Navigating the City:** York is a compact city with narrow streets and a historic layout, making it less suitable for driving within the city center. Many areas are pedestrianized, and parking can be limited.
2. **Traffic Restrictions:** Be aware of the York City Center Traffic Management Scheme, which

restricts access to certain areas for non-residents. Familiarize yourself with signage to avoid fines.
3. **Parking:** Look for designated parking areas and understand parking regulations. Consider using Park and Ride facilities if you plan to explore the city center extensively.

Exploring Beyond York

Having a car opens up many possibilities for day trips and exploring the stunning Yorkshire countryside:

1. **Yorkshire Dales National Park:** A little over an hour's drive from York, this national park offers breathtaking landscapes, hiking trails, and charming villages.
2. **Whitby:** A seaside town known for its historic abbey and beautiful beaches, approximately 1.5 hours from York.
3. **Castle Howard:** A magnificent stately home located just 30 minutes from York, perfect for a day of exploration.
4. **Harrogate and Knaresborough:** Both are lovely towns just over an hour away, known for their spa heritage and stunning scenery.

Returning the Car

1. **Return Location:** Ensure you know where to return your car, especially if you rented it from an airport or specific location.

2. **Condition Check:** Before returning, check the car for any damage or belongings. Taking photos of the car can help in case of disputes regarding the vehicle's condition.
3. **Fuel:** Remember to refuel if your rental agreement requires a full-to-full return.

Final Tips

1. **Plan Your Routes:** Use GPS or a navigation app to help you find your way, especially when driving in unfamiliar areas.
2. **Stay Safe:** Follow UK driving regulations, including driving on the left-hand side of the road and adhering to speed limits.
3. **Consider Alternatives:** If your primary focus is exploring York, consider using public transportation, taxis, or cycling for city travel, reserving the rental car for day trips.

Renting a car in York can enhance your travel experience, providing you the freedom to explore not only the city but also the beautiful landscapes and historic sites of Yorkshire at your own pace.

3.4 Biking and Walking

York is a compact and pedestrian-friendly city, making it an ideal destination for both biking and walking. With its rich history, charming streets, and picturesque scenery, exploring York on foot or by bike allows you to soak in the sights at a leisurely pace. Here's everything you need to know about biking and walking in York.

Walking in York

Walking is one of the best ways to experience the beauty and history of York. The city is filled with historic landmarks, quaint shops, and scenic views, all easily accessible by foot.

Key Walking Routes

1. **City Walls:** The medieval city walls offer a unique vantage point and a picturesque walk around the city. The full circuit is about 2 miles long and provides stunning views of the Minster, river, and surrounding areas.
2. **The Shambles:** One of York's most famous streets, The Shambles is a narrow, cobbled lane lined with medieval buildings, shops, and cafes. It's a must-visit for anyone exploring York on foot.
3. **River Ouse Path:** The path along the River Ouse offers a peaceful walking route. You can enjoy scenic views of the water, historic buildings, and wildlife.
4. **Museum Gardens:** Located near the city center, these beautiful gardens are perfect for a leisurely stroll. You can enjoy the floral displays, the ruins of St. Mary's Abbey, and views of the nearby Yorkshire Museum.

Walking Tours

1. **Guided Tours:** Various companies offer guided walking tours that delve into York's rich history, including ghost tours, literary tours, and food tours.
2. **Self-Guided Tours:** You can find self-guided walking tour maps at visitor information centers or online, allowing you to explore at your own pace.

Accessibility

York is largely accessible for walkers, though some cobbled streets may present challenges for those with mobility issues. Many attractions are located close together, making it easy to see the city without extensive travel.

Biking in York

Biking is another fantastic way to explore York and its surroundings. The city has embraced cycling, offering dedicated paths and bike-friendly routes.

Bike Rental Options

1. **Local Rental Shops:** Several shops in York offer bike rentals, including Cycle Heaven and York Cycle Hire, where you can choose from a range of bikes, including traditional bikes, electric bikes, and family options.

2. **Bike Sharing:** Some bike-sharing programs are available, allowing you to rent bikes for short trips. Check local resources for details.

Cycling Routes

1. **Dedicated Bike Paths:** York has many dedicated bike paths and lanes that make cycling safe and enjoyable. Look for signs indicating bike routes.
2. **The Solar System Cycle Route:** A unique, educational cycling route that takes you through the solar system, with scale models of the planets placed along the route. It's a fun and informative ride for families and individuals.
3. **York to Selby Cycle Path:** This route runs alongside the River Ouse and offers a scenic ride to the nearby town of Selby, about 10 miles from York.

Cycling Events and Clubs

1. **York Cycle Rally:** An annual event that celebrates cycling in York, featuring rides, stalls, and activities for cyclists of all ages and abilities.
2. **Local Cycling Clubs:** Joining a local cycling club can enhance your experience, providing opportunities for group rides and socializing with fellow cycling enthusiasts.

Safety and Tips

1. **Wear a Helmet:** Although not legally required for adults, wearing a helmet is strongly recommended for safety.
2. **Be Aware of Traffic:** While York is bike-friendly, be mindful of other road users, especially in busy areas. Follow cycling rules and signals.
3. **Lock Your Bike:** Use a sturdy lock to secure your bike when parked. There are designated bike racks throughout the city.

Whether you choose to explore York on foot or by bike, both options offer unique perspectives on this historic city. Walking allows you to leisurely enjoy the sights, while biking provides a bit more speed and the chance to venture further afield. Both methods of transportation are eco-friendly, making them ideal choices for the environmentally conscious traveler. Embrace the charm of York as you discover its hidden gems and vibrant atmosphere at your own pace!

Chapter 4: Exploring Historical Treasures

Exploring the historical treasures of York is a journey through time, where every cobblestone street, medieval building, and ancient artifact tells a story. Here's a guide to help you uncover some of the city's most remarkable historical sites and attractions:

4.1 The Shambles: A Medieval Marvel

One of the most iconic and enchanting streets in York, the Shambles, is a living testament to the city's medieval history. This winding, narrow lane is often described as a time capsule that transports visitors back in time, evoking the sights and sounds of a bygone era. The Shambles is not merely a street; it's a living piece of history, a bustling hub of activity, and a must-visit destination for anyone exploring York.

- **A Glimpse into the Past:** The Shambles, with its overhanging timber-framed buildings, uneven cobblestones, and leaning facades, offers a glimpse into what York would have looked like during the Middle Ages. The street's history dates back over 900 years, and its

original purpose was as a market street where butchers would sell their wares.
- **Distinctive Architecture:** What sets the Shambles apart is its unique architectural style. The buildings are so close together at the top that they almost touch, creating a tunnel-like effect. As you stroll along the cobblestones, you'll notice the leaning facades, which were intentionally designed this way to allow upper floors to extend over the street, providing shelter to those below.
- **Exploring the Shambles:** Today, the Shambles is lined with a charming array of shops, boutiques, cafes, and souvenir stores. You can find everything from traditional sweet shops to modern fashion boutiques, making it a delightful place to shop for gifts or simply soak in the atmosphere. The street's original purpose as a meat market is still evident in the names of some of the shops.
- **Photographic Opportunity:** Photographers and history enthusiasts alike will find the Shambles a captivating subject. The street's crooked, leaning buildings, flower-adorned window boxes, and atmospheric lighting create a picture-perfect scene that transports you back in time.

Tips for Visiting:

- **Timing:** To experience the Shambles without the crowds, consider visiting early in the morning or during the late afternoon.

- **Weekdays:** Weekdays are generally less busy than weekends, offering a more relaxed experience.
- **Explore:** Don't just walk the main thoroughfare; explore the narrow alleyways and hidden corners to discover charming nooks.
- **Mind the Space:** Due to the narrowness of the street, be mindful of fellow visitors and shop owners.
- **History:** Take a moment to appreciate the historic plaques and information boards that provide insights into the street's history.

4.2 York Minster: Iconic Gothic Cathedral

Standing majestically at the heart of York, York Minster is a masterpiece of architecture, a symbol of faith, and a testament to the city's rich history. This magnificent Gothic cathedral has drawn pilgrims, tourists, and admirers for centuries, and its towering spires and intricate design make it one of the most iconic landmarks in the United Kingdom. Let's delve into the splendor of York Minster:

A Triumph of Gothic Architecture

York Minster's construction began in the 13th century and took several centuries to complete. Its architectural style is predominantly Gothic, characterized by soaring pointed arches, elaborate carvings, and stunning stained glass windows. The cathedral's architecture reflects the evolution of Gothic design, incorporating both Early English and Perpendicular styles.

Key Features

- **Towers and Spires:** York Minster boasts two impressive towers – the northwestern "Mary" Tower and the southwestern "Peter" Tower. The central tower, a magnificent example of English Gothic architecture, offers breathtaking panoramic views of the city.
- **Rose Window:** The Great East Window, also known as the "Heart of Yorkshire," is the largest expanse of medieval stained glass in the world. Its intricate design and vibrant colors tell the story of creation, redemption, and the Last Judgment.
- **Chapter House:** The Chapter House features a stunning octagonal design with intricate vaulting and a central pillar. It's a testament to the medieval craftsmen's skill and attention to detail.

Visiting York Minster

- **Guided Tours:** Joining a guided tour can provide in-depth insights into the cathedral's history, architecture, and significance. Experienced tour guides tell amusing tales and anecdotes that bring the cathedral to life.

- **Tower Climb:** Climbing the central tower's narrow spiral staircase is rewarded with awe-inspiring views of the city. It's a bit of a climb, but the experience is well worth it.
- **Worship Services:** York Minster is still a place of worship, and attending a service can be a moving experience. Check the schedule for services and choral performances.

Legacy and Significance

York Minster's towering spires and intricate details are not only a feast for the eyes but also a testament to human creativity and devotion. It stands as a representation of York's spiritual heritage and architectural prowess, offering visitors a chance to connect with the past, marvel at artistic achievements, and experience the sublime beauty of Gothic architecture in all its glory.

Tips for Visiting

- **Early Arrival:** Arrive early in the day to explore before the crowds arrive. This allows you to enjoy the interior in a more serene atmosphere.
- **Photography:** Photography is allowed inside the cathedral, but be mindful of others and the sacredness of the space.
- **Visitor Center:** The Minster's visitor center offers information, exhibits, and a gift shop where you can learn more about its history and architecture.

- **Respectful Attire:** Remember that York Minster is a place of worship. Dress modestly and be respectful of those who come to pray.

4.3 Clifford's Tower and York Castle

Perched on a grassy mound overlooking the city, Clifford's Tower and its surroundings are steeped in history and intrigue. This iconic landmark, part of the larger York Castle complex, holds tales of power, conflict, and resilience that span centuries. Let's uncover the significance of Clifford's Tower and the history of York Castle:

Clifford's Tower

- **Origins and Purpose:** Clifford's Tower was originally built by William the Conqueror in the 11th century as a symbol of his authority over the city. Its strategic location allowed for a commanding view of York and its surrounding landscape.
- **History and Transformations:** Throughout its history, Clifford's Tower has served various purposes, including as a royal residence, treasury, and prison. It was later associated with tragic events, including the massacre of Jewish residents in 1190.
- **Present-day Experience:** Today, visitors can explore Clifford's Tower, climb to its top for

panoramic views of York, and learn about its history through informational displays. The tower is managed by English Heritage.

York Castle

- **Historical Context:** York Castle consisted of more than just Clifford's Tower; it encompassed a complex of buildings, including a bailey and other defensive structures. The castle played a crucial role in the defense of the city over the centuries.
- **Role in Law and Justice:** The castle was a center of justice, with courts held within its walls. Trials, executions, and legal proceedings were carried out here, contributing to its reputation as a place of both power and punishment.
- **Subsequent Changes:** Over time, various parts of the castle were demolished or repurposed, altering its original appearance. The castle's role in the legal system diminished, and it gradually transitioned into a symbol of York's historical heritage.
- **Present-day Significance:** While much of the original castle complex no longer stands, Clifford's Tower remains a prominent and evocative reminder of York's medieval history. Its position offers visitors a glimpse into the city's layout and its importance throughout the ages.

Tips for Visiting

- **Historical Insights:** Engage with informational displays and interpretive signage on-site to understand the tower's history and its role in York's past.
- **Panoramic Views:** Don't miss the opportunity to climb to the top of Clifford's Tower for panoramic views of York's skyline and the surrounding countryside.
- **Explore Surroundings:** While Clifford's Tower is the focal point, take time to explore the tower's surroundings, including the remnants of the castle's bailey.
- **Check Opening Hours:** Ensure you're aware of Clifford's Tower's opening hours and any admission fees, especially if you plan to enter the tower.

Visiting Clifford's Tower and York Castle offers a window into the city's history, from its Norman beginnings to its role in medieval society. It's a chance to stand where generations before you have stood, to reflect on the events that shaped York's past, and to appreciate the significance of this enduring landmark in the heart of the city.

4.4 Jorvik Viking Centre: Unveiling Viking History

Step into the captivating world of Viking history at the Jorvik Viking Centre in York. This immersive attraction takes visitors on a journey back in time to the days when Vikings roamed the streets of the city, offering a unique and interactive experience that brings the past to life. Here's a glimpse into what the Jorvik Viking Centre has to offer:

Recreating Viking York

- **Interactive Exhibits:** The Jorvik Viking Centre is known for its interactive exhibits that recreate the sights, sounds, and even smells of Viking-age York. The attraction is built over the site of an archaeological dig that uncovered the remains of a Viking settlement, allowing visitors to step directly into the past.
- **Ride Experience:** The centerpiece of the Jorvik Viking Centre is a ride that takes you on a journey through a reconstructed Viking village. As you glide through the scenes, you'll witness the daily lives of the inhabitants, from traders and craftsmen to families and warriors.
- **Sights and Sounds:** The attention to detail is astonishing, with animatronic figures, authentic smells, and informative displays that transport you to another era. It's a multi-sensory experience that offers a vivid understanding of Viking society.

Learning and Engagement

- **Educational Insights:** Throughout the exhibits, you'll find informative displays that shed light on Viking history, culture, and traditions. Learn about their settlements, trading networks, and contributions to the development of York.
- **Archaeological Discoveries:** The attraction also showcases archaeological discoveries made during the dig, giving you a glimpse into the tangible artifacts that tell the story of Viking life in York.
- **Hands-On Activities:** The Jorvik Viking Centre often features interactive activities and workshops, allowing visitors to try their hand at Viking crafts, learn about Viking clothing, and more.

Cultural Connection

The Jorvik Viking Centre offers a profound connection to York's Viking heritage. It's an experience that not only educates but also immerses you in the past, allowing you to appreciate the history, achievements, and challenges of the people who once called this city home. Through interactive exhibits and engaging storytelling, the Jorvik Viking Centre transforms history from a distant concept into a tangible and memorable adventure.

Planning Your Visit

- **Tickets:** Purchase your tickets in advance, especially during peak tourist seasons, to secure your preferred entry time.
- **Duration:** Plan for at least a couple of hours to fully explore the exhibits and enjoy the ride experience.
- **Family-Friendly:** The Jorvik Viking Centre is family-friendly, making it a great choice for visitors of all ages.
- **Souvenirs:** Don't forget to visit the gift shop, where you can find Viking-inspired souvenirs, books, and unique mementos.

4.5 York City Walls: A Stroll through Time

Embark on a journey through centuries of history as you walk along the ancient York City Walls. These impressive fortifications encircle the heart of the city, offering not only a unique perspective on York's past but also stunning views of its present. Here's why a stroll along the city walls is an essential part of any visit to York:

Historical Significance

- **Roman Origins:** The origins of York's city walls can be traced back to Roman times when the city was known as Eboracum. The Romans

built the initial fortifications to protect the strategic settlement.
- **Medieval Evolution:** The walls were later expanded and strengthened during medieval times, reflecting York's growing importance as a political, economic, and cultural hub.

Glimpses of the Past

As you walk along the city walls, you'll encounter towers, gatehouses, and sections of the walls that offer glimpses into York's past:

- **Bootham Bar:** This well-preserved gateway offers a fascinating mix of Roman, medieval, and Victorian architecture.
- **Clifford's Tower:** The walls provide impressive views of Clifford's Tower, another iconic York landmark.
- **Micklegate Bar:** Once a major entrance to the city, this gatehouse boasts a history rich in royal processions and political symbolism.

Stunning Views

- **Skyline Panoramas:** Walking the walls provides you with panoramic views of York's skyline, including the towering spires of York Minster and the historic cityscape below.
- **River Ouse:** The walls also overlook the serene River Ouse, offering picturesque scenes of boats gliding along the water.

Hidden Gems

- **Gardens and Parks:** The walls lead you past hidden gardens and green spaces, such as the Museum Gardens, providing moments of tranquility amidst the urban landscape.
- **Local Flair:** Along the walls, you might encounter buskers, artists, and performers who contribute to the vibrant atmosphere of the city.

A Walk Through Time

Walking along the York City Walls is more than just a stroll; it's a walk through time, a chance to connect with the city's past, and an opportunity to appreciate the architectural feats of those who came before us. It's a reminder that while the world around us changes, the walls continue to stand as silent witnesses to the stories, events, and lives that have shaped the city into the vibrant and historical treasure that it is today.

Tips for Your Walk

- **Comfortable Shoes:** Wear comfortable walking shoes, as the walls have uneven surfaces and steps.
- **Weather Preparedness:** Be prepared for varying weather conditions, as parts of the walls are exposed to the elements.
- **Photography:** Don't forget your camera or smartphone to capture the breathtaking views and historic landmarks.

- **Direction:** The walls are typically walked in a clockwise direction. Follow signs and maps to stay on the path.

4.6 Treasurer's House and Its Ghostly Tales

Nestled within the heart of York, the Treasurer's House is not only a beautifully preserved historic townhouse but also a place shrouded in mystery and ghostly tales. This enchanting property offers a glimpse into the past, with its exquisite interiors and manicured gardens, while its haunted reputation adds an element of intrigue and excitement to any visit.

Historical Splendor

- **Origins:** The Treasurer's House dates back to the 17th century and was built by the wealthy merchant and collector Frank Green. Its architecture showcases the opulence of the period, with elegant rooms and ornate details that provide a window into York's past.
- **Interior Design:** The house's interiors are adorned with period-appropriate furnishings, artwork, and décor, offering a glimpse into the refined tastes of its former inhabitants.

Ghostly Legends

- **Roman Soldiers:** One of the most famous ghostly tales associated with the Treasurer's House is that of Roman soldiers. Legend has it that an ancient Roman road runs beneath the property, and visitors have reported sightings of ghostly legionnaires marching through the basement.
- **Ghosts of the Plague:** Another haunting tale involves the apparitions of a group of individuals dressed in 17th-century clothing, believed to be victims of the plague. The story suggests that these spirits move through the house, reenacting a scene from the past.

Paranormal Investigations

- **Harry Martindale:** Harry Martindale, a plumber who worked at the Treasurer's House, claimed to have encountered the ghostly Roman soldiers during routine repairs in the cellar. His experience sparked widespread interest in the house's haunted reputation.
- **Investigations:** Over the years, paranormal investigators and enthusiasts have explored the Treasurer's House, using equipment and techniques to detect any supernatural activity. Some visitors have reported strange sensations, unexplained sounds, and even ghostly sightings.

Visitor Experience

- **Guided Tours:** Joining a guided tour of the Treasurer's House allows you to learn about its history, its former occupants, and the ghostly legends that surround it.
- **Gardens:** The beautifully landscaped gardens offer a tranquil escape and a chance to explore the outdoor spaces that complement the house's charm.
- **Atmosphere:** The Treasurer's House's carefully preserved interiors and authentic ambiance make it a unique place to immerse yourself in the past, whether you're interested in its history or its ghostly tales.

A Tapestry of Time and Mystery

The Treasurer's House weaves a tapestry of history, elegance, and enigma. Whether you're drawn by its historical significance, its beautifully preserved interiors, or its ghostly tales, a visit to the Treasurer's House is an opportunity to step into the past and connect with the layers of stories that have left their mark on this captivating York treasure.

Tips for Your Visit

- **Booking:** Check the official website for guided tours, opening hours, and admission fees .
- **Ghost Hunts:** If you're intrigued by the ghostly legends, keep an eye out for special events, such as ghost hunts,

Chapter 5: Cultural Delights

York is a city that offers a rich tapestry of cultural experiences, from its historic landmarks to its artistic expressions. Immerse yourself in a diverse range of cultural delights that capture the essence of this enchanting city.

5.1 York's Thriving Arts and Music Scene

York's cultural landscape is alive with artistic expression and musical vibrancy, offering a dynamic and diverse range of experiences for residents and visitors alike. Immerse yourself in the city's thriving arts and music scene to witness the harmonious blend of tradition and innovation:

1. **Live Music Venues**
   - **The Crescent Community Venue:** A hub for live music, this versatile space hosts gigs, club nights, and community events, embracing a wide range of genres.
   - **Fibbers:** A legendary music venue that has hosted both emerging artists and established bands, presenting an eclectic mix of live performances.
   - **The Basement:** This intimate space showcases local talent, featuring live music, open mic nights, and DJ sets.

2. **Classical Music and Choirs**
   - **York Minster:** Attend concerts within the majestic confines of York Minster, where choirs and orchestras deliver captivating performances.
   - **University of York Concerts:** Enjoy classical concerts, recitals, and performances by visiting artists at the University of York's music department.
3. **Contemporary Art Spaces**
   - **York Art Gallery:** Discover an array of contemporary artworks, participate in workshops, and engage with the ever-changing exhibitions that highlight modern creativity.
   - **According to McGee:** An independent art gallery showcasing contemporary art and hosting exhibitions, talks, and art-related events.
4. **Theatre and Drama**
   - **York Theatre Royal:** Experience a wide range of theatrical productions, from classic plays to modern works, performed by talented actors.
   - **Joseph Rowntree Theatre:** A community theater offering diverse performances, including plays, musicals, and dance shows.
5. **Festivals and Cultural Events**
   - **York Festival of Ideas:** Celebrate innovative ideas, engaging discussions, and cultural exploration through lectures, workshops, and performances.

- **York Mediale:** A digital arts festival that showcases groundbreaking installations, multimedia experiences, and interactive artworks.
6. **Cultural Spaces**
- **York Explore Library and Archives:** Engage with literary events, workshops, and exhibitions in this modern library, fostering a love for literature and creativity.
- **York St. Mary's:** A contemporary art space housed within a medieval church, offering exhibitions that juxtapose modern artworks against historical architecture.
7. **Local Bands and Emerging Artists:** As you explore York's streets, you may encounter local musicians, artists, and street performers adding to the vibrant atmosphere.
8. **Cultural Collaborations:** York's artists often collaborate across disciplines, from musicians collaborating with visual artists to theater companies merging with dance troupes.

5.2 The Theatre Royal and Grand Opera House

In the heart of York's cultural scene, the Theatre Royal and Grand Opera House stand as two iconic venues that have entertained audiences for generations. These theaters not only showcase a variety of performances but also embody the city's appreciation for the arts, drama, and live entertainment. Let's take a closer look at these theatrical treasures:

Theatre Royal: A Historic Gem

- **History and Significance:** The Theatre Royal, dating back to 1744, is one of the oldest continuously operating theaters in the country. Its rich history includes hosting performances by acclaimed actors, playwrights, and musicians over the centuries.
- **Architectural Splendor:** The theater's elegant Georgian architecture adds to its allure, creating an atmosphere of timeless sophistication.
- **Performances:** The Theatre Royal hosts a diverse range of productions, including plays, musicals, comedies, and dance performances. Its varied program caters to audiences of all ages and tastes.
- **Community Engagement:** The theater is deeply involved in the local community, offering educational programs, workshops, and initiatives that encourage participation in the performing arts.

Grand Opera House: Majestic Entertainment

- **Historic Venue:** The Grand Opera House, built in 1902, exudes grandeur and opulence. Its Edwardian architecture and lavish interiors

transport visitors to an era of theatrical elegance.
- **Variety of Performances:** The Grand Opera House showcases a wide array of performances, from West End musicals and drama to comedy acts and live music concerts.
- **Cultural Heritage:** The theater's rich history is woven into the fabric of York's cultural heritage, making it a beloved destination for both locals and visitors.
- **Diverse Audiences:** The Grand Opera House's diverse program ensures there's something for everyone, making it an accessible and welcoming space for all theater enthusiasts.

Embracing the Magic of Theatre

The Theatre Royal and Grand Opera House are more than just venues; they are gateways to a world of imagination, emotion, and creativity. Whether you're captivated by a stirring drama, swept away by a musical, or enthralled by a comedy, these theaters offer an opportunity to experience the transformative power of live performance. York's theatrical treasures are a testament to the enduring allure of the stage and the city's commitment to preserving and celebrating the art of entertainment.

Tips for Enjoying the Theaters

- **Booking Tickets:** Check the official websites of the Theatre Royal and Grand Opera House

for show listings, performance dates, and ticket availability.
- **Arrive Early:** Arriving early allows you to explore the theater's architecture and soak in the pre-show ambiance.
- **Parking and Accessibility:** Consider using public transportation or nearby parking facilities, as both theaters are conveniently located in the city center.
- **Student and Group Discounts:** Check for special rates, discounts, and offers, especially if you're attending with a group or are a student.

5.3 York Art Gallery: A Collection of Artistic Gems

Nestled within the historic city of York, the York Art Gallery stands as a cultural treasure trove, inviting visitors to explore a diverse array of artworks that span centuries and genres. With its impressive collection, engaging exhibitions, and immersive experiences, the gallery serves as a vibrant hub for artistic appreciation and cultural enrichment. Let's delve into the captivating world of the York Art Gallery:

Exquisite Collections

- **Historical and Contemporary Art:** The gallery's collection encompasses artworks from the 14th century to contemporary pieces,

offering a comprehensive view of artistic evolution over the ages.
- **Paintings and Sculptures:** Discover an eclectic mix of paintings, sculptures, decorative arts, and objects that reflect various artistic movements and styles.
- **Victorian Art:** The gallery boasts one of the finest collections of Victorian art in the country, featuring works by renowned artists such as Turner, Constable, and more.
- **Contemporary Exhibitions:** York Art Gallery is not only a repository of historical art but also a platform for contemporary artists to showcase their creations, fostering a dynamic connection between the past and the present.

Engaging Experiences

- **Center of Learning:** The gallery is a hub of education and inspiration, offering workshops, talks, and interactive activities that cater to art enthusiasts of all ages.
- **Curated Exhibitions:** Special exhibitions are held throughout the year, offering fresh perspectives on specific artists, movements, and themes. These exhibits often feature pieces on loan from other institutions, adding to the diversity of the gallery's offerings.
- **Challenging Perspectives:** The gallery is committed to challenging traditional narratives and exploring diverse perspectives through its

exhibitions, contributing to ongoing dialogues about art, society, and culture.

Stunning Architecture

- **Grand Gallery:** The recently renovated Grand Gallery is an architectural marvel that seamlessly blends historical features with contemporary design. It contains a substantial collection of ornamental arts, sculptures, and paintings.
- **Cozy Courtyard:** The gallery's delightful courtyard provides a serene space for relaxation, reflection, and contemplation amidst the bustling city.

A Journey Through Artistic Expression

The York Art Gallery is a testament to the power of artistic expression to transcend time, communicate ideas, and capture the human experience. As you walk through its halls, you'll encounter a vibrant tapestry of creativity that reflects the essence of different eras, styles, and voices. Whether you're an art aficionado or a curious explorer, the York Art Gallery promises an enriching experience that celebrates the beauty, diversity, and significance of visual art in all its forms.

Practical Information

- **Opening Hours:** Check the official website for the latest information on opening hours and any special exhibitions.
- **Admission Fees:** Admission charges may apply, with concessions available for students, seniors, and families.
- **Accessibility:** The gallery is committed to ensuring accessibility for all visitors. Check for information on facilities and services for those with specific needs.
- **Guided Tours:** Consider joining guided tours to gain deeper insights into the artworks, their historical context, and the gallery's highlights.

5.4 Festivals and Events Calendar

York is a city that comes alive with a diverse range of festivals and events throughout the year, each offering a unique opportunity to immerse yourself in the city's culture, history, and vibrant atmosphere. Here's a glimpse into the exciting festivals and events calendar in York:

January

- **York Residents Festival:** An annual event where locals can explore their city's attractions and landmarks for free or at discounted rates.

February

- **Jorvik Viking Festival:** A week-long celebration of Viking heritage, featuring reenactments, workshops, talks, and activities that transport you back in time.

March

- **York Literature Festival:** A literary extravaganza featuring author talks, workshops, discussions, and poetry readings that celebrate the written word.

April

- **York Chocolate Festival:** Indulge in all things chocolate-related, from tastings and demonstrations to workshops and chocolate-themed events.

May

- **York International Shakespeare Festival:** A biennial festival celebrating the works of William Shakespeare with performances, workshops, and discussions.

June

- **Bloom! York Festival:** Enjoy the beauty of spring with flower displays, gardening workshops, and horticultural events across the city.

July

- **Great Yorkshire Fringe:** A diverse arts festival featuring comedy, theater, music, cabaret, and more in various venues around the city.

August

- **Yorkshire Day:** Celebrate all things Yorkshire with special events, performances, and activities that highlight the region's unique culture.
- **York Food and Drink Festival:** A culinary extravaganza celebrating local and international cuisine, with food stalls, cooking demonstrations, and tastings.

September

- **York Mediale:** A digital arts festival that showcases innovative installations, interactive artworks, and multimedia experiences.

October

- **Illuminating York:** A stunning light festival that transforms historic sites and landmarks with breathtaking light displays and projections.

November

- **St. Nicholas' Fair:** York's traditional Christmas market, offering festive stalls, crafts, gifts, and seasonal treats.

December

- **York Early Music Christmas Festival:** Enjoy concerts and performances that transport you to the music of bygone eras in historic venues.
- **Festival of Angels:** A magical event where the city is adorned with illuminated angels, creating a whimsical atmosphere.

Ongoing Events

- **Ghost Walks:** Year-round, explore the city's haunted history with guided ghost walks that lead you through York's dark and mysterious past.
- **Museums and Galleries:** Many of York's museums and galleries host rotating exhibitions, workshops, and events throughout the year.
- **Live Music:** Local venues offer live music performances, covering a range of genres from classical to contemporary.

Plan Your Visit

When planning your visit to York, check the official websites of these festivals and events for up-to-date information on dates, schedules, and any ticket requirements. Whether you're interested in history, art, food, or music, York's festivals and events calendar ensures that there's something captivating happening in the city every month of the year.

5.5 Exploring York's Literature Connections

York's cobblestone streets, historic buildings, and rich cultural heritage have inspired countless writers, poets, and storytellers throughout history. Immerse yourself in the city's literary connections as you follow in the footsteps of literary greats and discover the places that have shaped their works:

1. **The Shambles: Inspiration for Diagon Alley**
   - **Literary Link:** J.K. Rowling is said to have drawn inspiration from York's charming and narrow medieval street, The Shambles when creating the magical Diagon Alley in the Harry Potter series.
   - **Experience:** Walk through The Shambles and imagine the bustling marketplace that inspired the iconic wizarding shopping district.

2. **York Explore Library and Archives:**
   - **Literary Hub:** This modern library hosts author talks, workshops, and literary events, nurturing a love for reading and writing within the community.
   - **Experience:** Attend a literary event, explore the library's extensive collection, and feel the creative energy that flows through the space.
3. **York Literature Festival:**
   - **Annual Celebration:** This festival brings together writers, poets, and literature enthusiasts for author talks, readings, and discussions, celebrating the written word.
   - **Experience:** Attend events featuring acclaimed authors, participate in workshops, and engage in conversations that delve into the world of literature.
4. **York St. Mary's: Literary and Art Fusion**
   - **Creative Space:** This contemporary art space within a medieval church often hosts exhibitions that merge visual art with literary themes, creating a unique fusion of creativity.
   - **Experience:** Explore exhibitions that blend visual and written expressions, offering a multi-dimensional experience of art and literature.
5. **Literary Walking Tours**
   - **Guided Tours:** Join a literary walking tour that takes you through the city's historic streets while sharing stories of famous authors, local legends, and literary landmarks.

- **Experience:** Discover the nooks and crannies that have inspired writers, and learn about the city's rich literary heritage from knowledgeable guides.
6. **The Ghostly Tales of York**
   - **Ghost Walks:** York's eerie atmosphere has inspired tales of the supernatural, making it a perfect backdrop for ghost walks and storytelling tours.
   - **Literary Inspiration:** Writers have woven the city's ghostly reputation into their stories, creating a unique blend of history and fiction.
   - **Experience:** Join a ghost walk tour to hear chilling tales that intertwine fact and fiction, adding a literary twist to your exploration.
7. **Hidden Gems and Quiet Corners:**
   - **Literary Escapes:** Seek out the city's hidden gardens, tranquil squares, and cozy cafes where writers may have found solace and inspiration.
   - **Experience:** Find a quiet spot to read or write, and let the city's ambiance fuel your imagination, just as it has for generations of writers.

York's literary connections are as varied as the genres they encompass. Whether you're a fan of classics, fantasy, history, or contemporary literature, the city's streets and spaces are infused with the stories of both celebrated authors and everyday wordsmiths. As you explore York's literary tapestry, you'll find that the magic of words and the allure of the city are interwoven in a way that invites you to embark on your literary journey.

5.6 Quaint Bookshops and Literary Sites

For book lovers and literary enthusiasts, York offers a treasure trove of quaint bookshops and literary sites that evoke a sense of nostalgia and wonder. From charming bookstores to historic sites that have inspired generations of writers, here's a guide to exploring the literary side of York:

1. **The Minster Gate Bookshop:** Tucked beside the majestic York Minster, this delightful bookshop specializes in second-hand and antiquarian books, creating an atmosphere of discovery and history. Browse through shelves filled with literary treasures, from classic novels to rare editions, and find a piece of literary history to take home.
2. **The Little Apple Bookshop:** This independent bookshop exudes a cozy and welcoming ambiance. Its knowledgeable staff and carefully curated selection make it a haven for book enthusiasts. Engage in conversations with passionate staff, attend book launches, and discover new reads in a warm and intimate setting.
3. **Barley Hall; A Medieval Experience:** Barley Hall, a reconstructed medieval

townhouse, offers a glimpse into life during the Middle Ages. It has been used as a setting for historical fiction events and activities. Immerse yourself in the past, and imagine the sights and sounds that could have inspired tales of knights, troubadours, and adventurers.

4. **Treasurer's House:** The Treasurer's House, known for its ghostly legends, offers a unique blend of history and mystery. Its haunted reputation has likely inspired many a tale. Explore the opulent interiors, learn about the house's history, and let the stories of the past spark your imagination.
5. **King's Manor Library; A Scholarly Retreat:** Situated within the King's Manor, a historic building once part of a monastery, this library provides a serene space for research, reading, and reflection. If you're a scholar or researcher, access the library's resources and soak in the scholarly atmosphere that has nurtured generations of academics.
6. **York Theatre Royal:** York Theatre Royal has hosted performances that have left an indelible mark on the literary landscape. Its historical significance adds to its allure. Attend a theatrical production, a play reading, or a literary event that bridges the worlds of drama and literature.
7. **Literary Walking Tours:** Join a literary walking tour that takes you to the city's literary landmarks, introducing you to the places that have inspired writers throughout history. Listen

to stories, anecdotes, and historical tidbits that bring the city's literary heritage to life as you walk its charming streets.
8. **Stone Trough Books:** It is a second-hand bookshop with a focus on antiquarian and rare books. It is located in a former mill on Walmgate, and it is a great place to find hidden gems.
9. **The Wordsworth Bookshop:** This is a large independent bookshop located in St. Helen's Square. It has a wide selection of books on all subjects, and it is a great place to spend a rainy afternoon.
10. **Stroll Through the Streets:** As you wander through York's winding streets, you'll find no shortage of cozy cafes, historic squares, and scenic corners where you can pause with a book. Carry a book with you, find a quiet spot, and let the city's atmosphere transport you into the pages of your chosen read.

Chapter 6: Culinary Journey Through York

York's culinary scene is a delightful blend of traditional Yorkshire fare, international cuisine, and modern gastronomy. As you explore the city's charming streets and historic landmarks, be sure to embark on a culinary journey that takes you from hearty pub grub to gourmet delights. Here's a taste of what York's diverse dining landscape has to offer:

6.1 Traditional Yorkshire Pudding and Roast Dinner

When it comes to hearty and comforting British cuisine, few dishes capture the essence of tradition and warmth quite like the Yorkshire pudding and roast dinner. Rooted in history and deeply loved by locals, this classic combination is a staple of Sunday lunches and festive meals. Let's dive into the delicious world of Yorkshire pudding and roast dinner:

Yorkshire Pudding

- **Origins:** While the exact origin of Yorkshire pudding is debated, it's widely believed to have originated in Yorkshire, England, as a way to

make a small amount of meat go further in a filling meal.
- **Characteristics:** Yorkshire pudding is a light and airy batter baked in the oven until it puffs up and becomes golden brown. It has a crispy exterior and a tender, slightly custardy interior.
- **Serving:** Traditionally, Yorkshire pudding is often served as a side dish with roast beef, but it can also accompany other roast meats like chicken, pork, or lamb.

Roast Dinner

- **Ingredients**: A traditional roast dinner typically consists of roasted meat, such as beef, lamb, chicken, or pork, served with roasted potatoes, seasonal vegetables, gravy, and of course, Yorkshire pudding.
- **Preparation:** The meat is slow-cooked to perfection, resulting in succulent and tender slices. Roasted potatoes are crispy on the outside and fluffy on the inside, and the vegetables add a burst of color and freshness to the plate.
- **Accompaniments:** A rich and flavorful gravy made from meat drippings enhances the meal, tying all the elements together.

Experience the Flavors:

- **Dining Out:** Many traditional British pubs and restaurants in York offer roast dinners as part of their Sunday lunch menus.

- **Home Cooking:** If you're staying in self-catering accommodation, you can create your roast dinner, complete with Yorkshire pudding, using local ingredients.

Taste of Tradition

- **Sunday Tradition:** The Sunday roast, including Yorkshire pudding, has long been a cherished tradition in British households, bringing families and friends together for a comforting meal.
- **Historical Significance:** The roast dinner and Yorkshire pudding have historical roots that date back centuries, reflecting the rich culinary heritage of Yorkshire and Britain as a whole.

Tips for Enjoying the Experience

- **Explore Pubs:** Seek out traditional pubs in York that specialize in serving classic British dishes, including roast dinners.
- **Pairing:** Yorkshire pudding and roast dinner pair wonderfully with a traditional British ale or a glass of red wine.
- **Appetite Required:** Be prepared for a hearty and satisfying meal that may leave you feeling delightfully full.
- **Variations:** While beef is the classic choice for roast dinners, feel free to explore other meat options based on your preferences.

Savor the Comfort

Yorkshire pudding and roast dinner encapsulate the heart and soul of British comfort food. When you take a bite of the tender meat, crispy potatoes, flavorful gravy, and that perfectly risen Yorkshire pudding, you're not only indulging in a delicious meal but also experiencing a taste of tradition and history that has stood the test of time.

6.2 The Famous Betty's Tea Room

Betty's Tea Room is a legendary institution that has been enchanting visitors and locals in York for nearly a century. With its elegant ambiance, delectable treats, and quintessentially British afternoon tea experience, Betty's Tea Room is a must-visit destination that captures the essence of both history and indulgence.

A Glimpse into Betty's Tea Room

Origins and Legacy: Betty's Tea Room was founded in 1919 by Frederick Belmont, a Swiss confectioner and baker. His vision was to create a place that combined the elegance of Switzerland with the traditional charm of Yorkshire.

Elegant Atmosphere: The tea room's interior exudes a timeless charm, featuring ornate woodwork, mirrored walls, and art deco touches that transport you to an era of refined sophistication.

Afternoon Tea: One of the highlights of Betty's Tea Room is its traditional afternoon tea, a ritual that celebrates the art of tea and indulgence. Served on delicate china, afternoon tea includes a selection of finger sandwiches, freshly baked scones with clotted cream and jam, and an assortment of cakes and pastries.

Specialty Teas: Betty's offers a wide range of teas, including classic blends, herbal infusions, and even some exclusive blends created by the tea experts at the establishment.

Famous Cakes and Pastries: Betty's is renowned for its exquisite selection of cakes, pastries, and chocolates. From delicate éclairs to rich chocolate tortes, every treat is crafted with precision and passion.

Locations

St. Helen's Square: This iconic Betty's location in the heart of York offers a charming tearoom experience where you can enjoy your afternoon tea or meal in elegant surroundings.

Harrogate: This Bettys Tea Room is located on Parliament Street in Harrogate.

Ilkley: This Bettys Tea Room is located in The Grove in Ilkley.

Northallerton: This Bettys Tea Room is located in Market Place in Northallerton

Tips for Visiting Betty's Tea Room:

Reservations: Given the popularity of Betty's, it's recommended to make a reservation, especially if you're planning to enjoy afternoon tea.

Attire: While there's no strict dress code, Betty's Tea Room offers an elegant atmosphere, and many visitors enjoy dressing up for the occasion.

Gift Shop: Explore the adjoining gift shops, where you can find an array of tea-related items, treats, and gifts to bring home as souvenirs.

Local Favorites: Don't miss the opportunity to try some of Betty's signature treats, such as the Fat Rascal—a currant-filled scone-like pastry—and the Swiss specialties that pay homage to the founder's heritage.

A Timeless Tradition

Betty's Tea Room is more than just a place to enjoy tea and treats; it's a window into a bygone era, where impeccable service, exquisite flavors, and an appreciation for the finer things in life converge. As you step into Betty's, you're transported to a world of elegance, where the simple act of sipping tea and savoring pastries becomes a cherished memory. Whether you're seeking a delightful afternoon tea experience or a taste of York's culinary heritage,

Betty's Tea Room promises an enchanting journey through taste and time.

6.3 Food Markets: Shambles Market, Newgate Market

In addition to its rich history and cultural attractions, York is known for its vibrant food markets that offer a diverse array of fresh produce, delectable treats, and local specialties. Two prominent food markets in the city, Shambles Market and Newgate Market, provide visitors with an opportunity to experience the culinary delights of York. Let's explore what these markets have to offer:

Shambles Market: A Historic Culinary Destination

- **Location:** Shambles Market is situated in the heart of the city, just off the historic Shambles Street.
- **Atmosphere:** This bustling market captures the essence of York's historical charm while offering a modern shopping experience.
- **Fresh Produce:** The market features stalls brimming with fresh fruits, vegetables, and herbs, allowing visitors to support local farmers and experience seasonal delights.

- **Street Food:** Indulge in a diverse range of street food options, from international flavors to traditional British favorites.
- **Artisanal Goods:** Browse through stalls offering artisanal bread, cheeses, meats, and deli items that showcase the region's culinary craftsmanship.
- **Cafés and Eateries:** Adjacent to the market, you'll find quaint cafés and eateries where you can relax and savor your market finds.

Newgate Market: A Hub of Flavors

- **Location:** Newgate Market is located in the city center, near Parliament Street and Coppergate.
- **Variety of Stalls:** This expansive market boasts a wide variety of stalls, including fresh produce, baked goods, clothing, crafts, and, of course, a delightful selection of food vendors.
- **Street Food Haven:** Explore the vibrant street food section, where you can sample cuisines from around the world, from Thai curries to gourmet burgers.
- **Market Ambiance:** Immerse yourself in the lively atmosphere as vendors interact with customers, sharing their passion for food and local products.
- **Local and International:** Newgate Market offers a blend of local Yorkshire products and

international flavors, making it a melting pot of culinary experiences.

Tips for Exploring the Markets

- **Timing:** Both markets are open throughout the week, but it's best to visit in the morning for the freshest produce and widest selection.
- **Exploration:** Take your time to stroll through the stalls, chat with vendors, and sample various foods to fully immerse yourself in the market experience.
- **Cash:** While many vendors accept card payments, it's advisable to carry some cash, especially for smaller purchases.
- **Market Days:** Both Shambles Market and Newgate Market operate daily,

Embrace the Flavors of York

Visiting Shambles Market and Newgate Market offers a glimpse into the vibrant culinary scene of York, where fresh produce, artisanal goods, and international cuisines come together. Whether you're seeking local ingredients for a self-catered meal, enjoying a quick bite of street food, or simply soaking in the market ambiance, these food markets are a vital part of York's cultural fabric and provide a delicious way to connect with the city's culinary heritage.

6.4 Exploring York's Chocolate Heritage

York's rich and delectable chocolate heritage is intertwined with its history, innovation, and passion for all things cocoa. From centuries-old chocolate houses to modern attractions dedicated to this indulgent treat, a journey through York's chocolate heritage is a must for any visitor with a sweet tooth and an appreciation for history. Here's how you can explore York's chocolate heritage:

- **York's Chocolate Story:** Visit York's Chocolate Story, an interactive attraction that takes you on a journey through the history of chocolate in York. Discover the origins of chocolate, the city's role in its development, and the stories behind famous chocolate brands. Participate in chocolate-making demonstrations and tastings, and even create your delicious treats.
- **Chocolate-Making Workshops:** Several chocolate shops in York offer chocolate-making workshops, where you can learn the art of crafting truffles, bars, and other confections. Join experienced chocolatiers who will guide you through the process, from tempering chocolate to adding fillings and decorations. At the end of the workshop, you'll get to take home your creations and enjoy the fruits of your chocolate-making efforts.

- **Chocolate Shops and Boutiques:** Wander down The Shambles, York's picturesque medieval street, where you'll find several chocolate shops and boutiques offering a variety of handcrafted chocolates. Indulge in a tempting selection of artisanal chocolates, truffles, pralines, and other delights created with love and care.
- **Chocolate Tasting Tours:** Join guided chocolate-tasting tours that take you to different chocolate shops in York, where you can sample a range of chocolates and learn about their flavors and origins. Some tours even offer chocolate pairings with wine, whiskey, or other beverages for a unique sensory experience.
- **Chocolate Festivals and Events:** Check if your visit coincides with one of York's chocolate festivals or events, where you can enjoy chocolate-themed activities, tastings, and even competitions. Immerse yourself in the city's chocolate culture as you explore stalls offering a diverse range of chocolate delights.
- **Discover the Cocoa Bean's Journey:** Learn about the journey of cocoa beans, from their origins in tropical countries to the chocolate-making process in York. Some attractions highlight the importance of ethical and sustainable sourcing of cocoa beans.

A Treat for All Ages

York's chocolate heritage isn't just for those with a sweet tooth—it's a journey through time, culture, and craftsmanship. Whether you're a history enthusiast, a chocolate connoisseur, or simply someone who appreciates a delicious treat, York's chocolate attractions and experiences promise to tantalize your senses, indulge your curiosity, and leave you with a deeper appreciation for the world of chocolate.

6.5 International and Fusion Cuisine

While York is steeped in history and tradition, its culinary scene also reflects the city's diversity and openness to global flavors. From international eateries to innovative fusion restaurants, York offers a delightful array of dining options that cater to a wide range of tastes. Embark on a global gastronomic adventure as you explore the international and fusion cuisine that York has to offer:

International Dining

1. **Indian Delights**
   - Mumbai Lounge: Enjoy authentic Indian cuisine with a modern twist, offering a diverse menu of curries, tandoori dishes, and more.

- Khao Pad: A contemporary restaurant that brings the flavors of Thailand to York, offering a menu of Thai classics and innovative creations.

2. **Italian Indulgence**
   - Sotano: This Italian-inspired restaurant features a tapas-style menu with dishes influenced by the flavors of Italy and the Mediterranean.
   - Delrio's Restaurant: Experience traditional Italian fare, from pasta to wood-fired pizzas, in a warm and welcoming atmosphere.

3. **Mediterranean Vibes**
   - Los Moros: Discover the vibrant flavors of North African and Middle Eastern cuisine, with dishes like tagines, falafel, and mezze platters.
   - Olive Tree Mediterranean Bistro: Immerse yourself in Mediterranean cuisine with a focus on fresh ingredients and traditional flavors.

Fusion Cuisine

1. **Balti Fusion**
   - **The Raj at the Bank:** A blend of Indian and Balti cuisine, offering a fusion of flavors that pay homage to the city's history.

2. **Modern Fusion**
   - **Skosh:** An innovative eatery that showcases a fusion of global flavors with British ingredients, resulting in creative small plates.

Global Street Food

- **Shambles Food Court:** Explore the Shambles Food Court for a diverse range of street food vendors offering everything from Japanese sushi to Mexican burritos.

Exotic Flavors

1. **Thai-influenced Fusion**
- The Whippet Inn: Experience a fusion of flavors that combines British ingredients with Thai influences for a unique dining experience.

Tips for Enjoying International and Fusion Cuisine:

- **Reservations:** Make reservations in advance, especially for popular fusion restaurants that offer unique culinary experiences.
- **Ask for Recommendations:** Don't hesitate to ask the staff for recommendations on dishes that best showcase the fusion of flavors.
- **Sharing Plates:** Many fusion eateries offer sharing plates or small plates, allowing you to try a variety of dishes in one sitting.
- **Be Adventurous:** Embrace the opportunity to try new and exciting flavor combinations that reflect the creativity of the chefs.

Chapter 7: Nature and Relaxation

While York is renowned for its historical landmarks and vibrant urban culture, it also offers serene pockets of nature and relaxation that provide a perfect escape from the bustling city streets. Whether you're seeking a stroll, a peaceful garden, or a calming waterfront, York has a variety of options to help you unwind and connect with nature.

7.1 Rowntree Park: Serene Riverside Escape

Nestled along the banks of the River Ouse, Rowntree Park is a hidden gem in the heart of York that offers a tranquil and picturesque retreat from the city's hustle and bustle. With its lush greenery, soothing waters, and peaceful ambiance, this park invites visitors to unwind, connect with nature, and enjoy moments of serenity. Here's what makes Rowntree Park a serene riverside escape:

- **Riverside Views:** Rowntree Park's location along the River Ouse provides visitors with stunning views of the tranquil waters. Whether you're sitting on a bench by the riverbank or strolling along the pathways, you'll be treated to

picturesque vistas that evoke a sense of calm and relaxation.
- **Lush Landscapes:** The park's well-maintained lawns, vibrant flower displays, and well-tended gardens create a lush and inviting environment. It's an ideal place for picnics, leisurely walks, or simply finding a quiet spot to read or meditate amidst nature's beauty.
- **Boating Lake:** The park features a serene boating lake, where you can watch ducks and swans gliding gracefully on the water. The lake adds to the park's peaceful ambiance and provides a charming focal point for visitors of all ages to enjoy.
- **Children's Playground:** For families visiting with children, Rowntree Park offers a well-equipped playground where kids can have fun and expend their energy. This ensures that the park is not only a serene retreat for adults but also a delightful destination for the little ones.
- **Café and Relaxation:** The Rowntree Park Reading Café is a cozy spot to relax and enjoy a cup of tea or coffee. Situated within the park, it offers a tranquil atmosphere and a chance to unwind while being surrounded by nature's beauty.
- **Community Feel:** Rowntree Park is beloved by both locals and visitors alike. The park's friendly and welcoming atmosphere creates a sense of community, making it a place where

people gather to relax, socialize, and enjoy the outdoors.
- **Historical Legacy:** Rowntree Park was gifted to the city of York by the Rowntree family in 1921, with the intention of providing a space for recreation and relaxation for the local community. The park's legacy of providing a serene escape remains true to this day.

Whether you're seeking a peaceful stroll, a riverside picnic, or a quiet place to sit and reflect, Rowntree Park offers a harmonious blend of natural beauty and a tranquil ambiance. It's a reminder that amidst the historical landmarks and urban activity, York also offers spaces for stillness and rejuvenation. Whether you're exploring on your own, spending time with loved ones, or simply seeking solace in nature, Rowntree Park is a serene riverside escape that invites you to slow down, breathe, and embrace the gentle rhythm of the river and the park's surroundings.

7.2 York Museum Gardens: Where History Meets Nature

Nestled in the heart of York, the York Museum Gardens offer a harmonious blend of historical intrigue and natural beauty. This serene and captivating space invites visitors to step back in time while enjoying the tranquility of lush landscapes. Let's explore why the York Museum Gardens is a unique destination where history and nature intertwine:

Historical Treasures

- **St. Mary's Abbey Ruins:** The focal point of the gardens is the hauntingly beautiful ruins of St. Mary's Abbey, which date back to the 11th century. These evocative remnants showcase the grandeur of medieval architecture and provide a window into York's historical past.
- **Roman Multangular Tower:** Another historical gem within the gardens is the Roman Multangular Tower, an ancient defensive structure that forms a fascinating connection to York's Roman heritage.
- **Georgian Mansion:** The gardens are also home to the Yorkshire Museum, housed in a Georgian-style mansion. The museum houses a diverse collection of artifacts, including archaeological finds, natural history specimens, and art.

Botanical Diversity

- **Lush Gardens:** In addition to its historical treasures, the gardens are a haven of natural beauty. Lush lawns, vibrant flowerbeds, and meandering paths invite visitors to explore and enjoy the serene surroundings.
- **Variety of Plants:** The gardens feature a wide variety of plant species, from colorful seasonal

blooms to carefully curated collections of trees and shrubs. This diversity adds to the gardens' appeal throughout the year.

Quiet Retreats

- **Peaceful Atmosphere:** The gardens provide an oasis of tranquility within the city, offering visitors a respite from the urban hustle and bustle.
- **Relaxation Spots:** Numerous benches and seating areas allow you to sit back and absorb the peaceful ambiance, whether you're reading a book, enjoying a picnic, or simply taking in the scenery.

Engaging Events

- **Outdoor Performances:** During the warmer months, the gardens come alive with outdoor performances, including theater productions, music events, and cultural festivals.
- **Educational Opportunities:** The gardens also host educational workshops, guided tours, and activities that cater to visitors of all ages, making it an engaging destination for families and curious minds.

The York Museum Gardens encapsulate the city's multifaceted character, seamlessly merging its historical legacy with the serenity of nature. As you wander through the gardens, you're not just experiencing an array of plant life and historical artifacts—you're connecting with the city's past, appreciating its present beauty, and creating your memories within its peaceful embrace. Whether you're exploring the abbey ruins, admiring the seasonal blooms, or simply finding a quiet spot to contemplate, the York Museum Gardens offer a unique space where history meets nature in a captivating and harmonious union.

7.3 Boat Cruises on the River Ouse

Exploring York from the vantage point of the River Ouse offers a unique and captivating perspective. Boat cruises along the river allow you to witness the city's historic landmarks, charming bridges, and scenic landscapes in a leisurely and picturesque manner. Whether you're seeking a peaceful escape or a guided tour filled with insights, the River Ouse boat cruises offer an unforgettable experience. Here's what you can expect:

1. Scenic Views and Landmarks
- **York Minster:** Sail past the iconic York Minster, the city's towering cathedral that stands as a testament to centuries of history and architectural brilliance.
- **City Walls and Bridges:** Enjoy the view of the medieval city walls and picturesque bridges that arch gracefully over the river, showcasing York's charming architecture.

- **Clifford's Tower:** Gaze upon Clifford's Tower, a historic landmark that offers a glimpse into York's medieval past, perched atop its mound.

2. *Guided Narration*

- **Historical Insights:** Many boat cruises offer guided narration, providing you with fascinating historical tidbits and stories about the landmarks and areas you pass by.
- **Local Lore:** Learn about the history of the River Ouse itself, including its role in trade, transportation, and York's development as a city.

3. *Sunset and Evening Cruises*

- **Romantic Atmosphere:** Sunset and evening cruises offer a romantic ambiance as the city's landmarks are bathed in the warm hues of the setting sun or illuminated by evening lights.
- **Relaxation and Serenity:** Experience the calming effect of the river's gentle currents and the quietude of the city as it winds down for the night.

4. *Choice of Cruises*

- **Standard Sightseeing Cruises:** These cruises typically last around 45 minutes to an hour and provide a comprehensive overview of the city's key landmarks.
- **Themed Cruises:** Some operators offer themed cruises, such as afternoon tea cruises, wine-tasting cruises, and even ghost-themed cruises for those who enjoy a touch of mystery.

5. **Boat Choices**
- **Traditional River Boats:** Step aboard traditional river boats that exude old-world charm and provide a sense of nostalgia.
- **Modern Comfort:** Some cruises are conducted on modern boats equipped with comfortable seating and amenities for a pleasant journey.

Tips for Enjoying Boat Cruises

- **Booking:** While some cruises allow walk-ins, it's recommended to book your tickets in advance, especially during peak tourist seasons.
- **Sun Protection:** If you're taking a daytime cruise, consider bringing sunglasses, sunscreen, and a hat to stay comfortable while out on the water.
- **Cameras:** Don't forget your camera or smartphone to capture the stunning views and landmarks from the river.
- **Dress Comfortably:** Wear comfortable clothing and footwear that allow you to move around the boat freely.

Embarking on a boat cruise along the River Ouse is an opportunity to see York from a different angle, where the historic architecture, natural landscapes, and calm waters combine to create a serene and enchanting atmosphere. Whether you're taking a daytime cruise to learn about the city's history or enjoying an evening cruise under the stars, the River Ouse boat cruises offer a unique and unforgettable way to immerse yourself in the beauty and charm of York.

7.4 Day Trips to the Yorkshire Dales

Escape the urban hustle and immerse yourself in the breathtaking landscapes of the Yorkshire Dales, a designated National Park renowned for its stunning scenery, charming villages, and outdoor adventures. Just a short drive from York, the Yorkshire Dales offer a perfect day trip opportunity to connect with nature and experience the beauty of the British countryside. What to anticipate on your day trip is as follows:

1. **Scenic Drives**
   - **Dramatic Landscapes:** As you drive through the Yorkshire Dales, you'll be greeted by rolling hills, expansive moorlands, and picturesque valleys that create a postcard-worthy panorama.
   - **Winding Roads:** The scenic routes wind through charming villages, offering glimpses of traditional stone-built cottages and centuries-old architecture.
2. **Hiking and Walking**
   - **Numerous Trails:** The Yorkshire Dales boasts an extensive network of hiking trails catering to all levels of hikers, from leisurely walkers to more experienced trekkers.

- **Ingleton Waterfalls Trail:** This circular trail takes you past a series of stunning waterfalls, making it a popular choice for nature enthusiasts.
- **Malham Cove:** Hike to the impressive Malham Cove, a natural limestone amphitheater that offers breathtaking views.

3. **Traditional Villages:**
- **Leyburn:** Explore charming villages like Leyburn, known for its local market and welcoming atmosphere.
- **Hawes:** Visit Hawes, home to the famous Wensleydale Creamery where you can sample and purchase the region's renowned cheese.

4. **Aysgarth Falls:**
- **Natural Beauty:** Aysgarth Falls is a set of stunning waterfalls where the River Ure tumbles over limestone steps, creating a picturesque and soothing setting.
- **Walking Trails:** Enjoy the marked walking trails that allow you to admire the falls from various viewpoints and immerse yourself in nature.

5. **Nature and Wildlife:**
- **Wildlife Spotting:** Keep an eye out for native wildlife such as red squirrels, birds of prey, and even wild deer that inhabit the Yorkshire Dales.
- **Rich Flora:** Depending on the time of year, you might encounter vibrant wildflowers and lush greenery that add to the region's allure.

6. **Local Pubs and Cafés**
- **Quaint Retreats:** Stop by local pubs and cafés to savor hearty British fare, traditional Yorkshire puddings, and perhaps even a refreshing pint.
- **Relaxation:** These charming establishments offer a cozy setting to rest your feet and enjoy a warm meal amidst the natural beauty.
7. **Photography Opportunities**
- **Capture the Beauty:** The Yorkshire Dales offer ample opportunities for photography, whether you're capturing the sweeping landscapes, cascading waterfalls, or the rustic charm of the villages.

Tips for Your Day Trip

- **Early Start:** Begin your day trip early to make the most of your time exploring the Yorkshire Dales' attractions and scenery.
- **Weather-Appropriate Clothing:** Wear comfortable clothing and sturdy footwear, and bring along weather-appropriate gear, especially if you plan to hike.
- **Snacks and Water:** Carry snacks and water to stay energized throughout the day, especially if you're planning to explore the trails.
- **Local Information:** Stop by the local visitor centers for maps, information on hiking trails, and recommendations on must-see spots.

A day trip to the Yorkshire Dales from York offers an opportunity to escape the city's buzz and immerse yourself in the tranquil and awe-inspiring landscapes of the British countryside. Whether you're hiking the trails, admiring waterfalls, or enjoying a leisurely drive through charming villages, the Yorkshire Dales promises a rejuvenating experience that celebrates the beauty and natural splendor of the region.

7.5 Biking and Hiking Trails

For outdoor enthusiasts and nature lovers, York, and its surrounding areas offer a plethora of biking and hiking trails that allow you to immerse yourself in the beauty of the landscape, from the lush countryside to charming villages. Whether you're an avid hiker, a leisurely cyclist, or somewhere in between, there's a trail for you to explore. Here are some notable options:

1. **York City Walls: Historic Stroll and Cycle**

The York City Walls offer a unique trail that allows you to walk or cycle along the medieval walls that encircle the city. Explore the historical landmarks and enjoy elevated views of the city while experiencing a blend of urban charm and outdoor adventure.

2. **York to Selby Cycle Route: Riverside Ride**

This scenic cycle route follows the River Ouse from York to the charming town of Selby. Enjoy the peaceful riverside scenery, pass through picturesque villages, and perhaps visit Selby Abbey and the local market town.

3. The Solar System Cycle Path: Celestial Exploration

This unique cycle path extends from York to Selby and is designed to scale the solar system, with each mile representing one million miles in reality. As you cycle, you'll encounter information panels about planets, providing an educational experience along with your outdoor adventure.

4. Sutton Bank National Park Centre: Majestic Views

The Sutton Bank National Park Centre offers a range of walking trails suitable for various levels of hikers. Hike up to the famous Sutton Bank viewpoint for breathtaking views over the Yorkshire Dales, with the iconic White Horse carved into the hillside.

5. Wheldrake Ings: Wetland Wander

This nature reserve offers easy walking trails that wind through wetlands, meadows, and woodland areas. Spot a variety of bird species and immerse yourself in the peaceful ambiance of the wetlands.

6. Yorkshire Wolds Way: Long-Distance Hiking

The Yorkshire Wolds Way is a long-distance footpath that traverses the scenic chalk landscape of the Yorkshire Wolds. Embark on a more substantial hiking adventure, enjoying panoramic views, tranquil valleys, and charming villages along the way.

7. Howardian Hills Circular Walk: Scenic Exploration

This circular walking route takes you through the picturesque Howardian Hills Area of Outstanding Natural Beauty. Encounter rolling hills, idyllic countryside, and charming villages, capturing the essence of rural Yorkshire.

8. Castle Howard Estate: Grand Grounds

Castle Howard's estate offers a range of walking and cycling trails that allow you to explore the vast grounds and enjoy the grandeur of the estate. Discover woodlands, lakes, and the stunning architecture of Castle Howard, a stately home and historic landmark.

1. Tips for Enjoying Trails:
- **Check Trail Conditions:** Before setting out, check for any trail updates or conditions,

especially if you're planning to hike or cycle longer routes.
- **Appropriate Gear:** Wear comfortable, weather-appropriate clothing and footwear. For longer hikes or bike rides, consider bringing essentials like water, snacks, and a map.
- **Local Information:** Utilize local visitor centers or online resources to gather information about trail options, difficulty levels, and directions.
- **Respect Nature:** Follow the principles of Leave No Trace by not disturbing wildlife, taking your trash with you, and staying on designated paths.

7.6 Relaxing Spas and Wellness Centers

When it comes to unwinding and rejuvenating, York offers a range of spas and wellness centers that provide the perfect setting for relaxation and self-care. From soothing massages to revitalizing treatments, these havens of tranquility allow you to escape the stresses of everyday life and indulge in a moment of serenity. Here are some of the top options for pampering yourself in York:

1. **Middlethorpe Spa; Historic Elegance:** This spa is located within the luxurious Middlethorpe Hall, this spa offers a blend of traditional and contemporary treatments in a

historic setting. Enjoy a range of treatments, including massages, facials, and holistic therapies, all designed to provide relaxation and rejuvenation. The spa's location within a 17th-century country house adds a touch of elegance to your wellness experience.
2. **The Grand, York; Urban Oasis:** The Grand Spa offers a variety of treatments, from classic massages to bespoke experiences tailored to your preferences. Indulge in the spa's rooftop hydrotherapy pool, where you can soak in warm waters while enjoying panoramic views of the city.
3. **Origins York:** Relaxing Retreat: Origins York offers an array of treatments, from massages to facials, ensuring you find the perfect way to unwind. Enjoy complimentary refreshments, including herbal teas, to complete your relaxation experience.
4. **The Spa at No.1:** This is a day spa located in a Georgian townhouse in the heart of York. It has a variety of treatments to choose from, as well as a swimming pool, a sauna, and a steam room.
5. **York Wellness Spa:** is a spa located in the heart of York, just a short walk from the Shambles. It has a variety of treatments to choose from, as well as a swimming pool, a sauna, and a steam room.

Tips for a Relaxing Spa Day:

- **Advance Booking:** Spa appointments can fill up quickly, so it's advisable to book your treatments in advance.
- **Arrive Early:** Arrive at the spa a little early to have time to change into a robe, unwind in the relaxation area, and prepare for your treatment.
- **Communication:** Communicate your preferences and any specific needs to your therapist to ensure your experience is tailored to your liking.
- **Hydration:** Drink plenty of water before and after your treatments to stay hydrated and maximize the benefits of your experience.

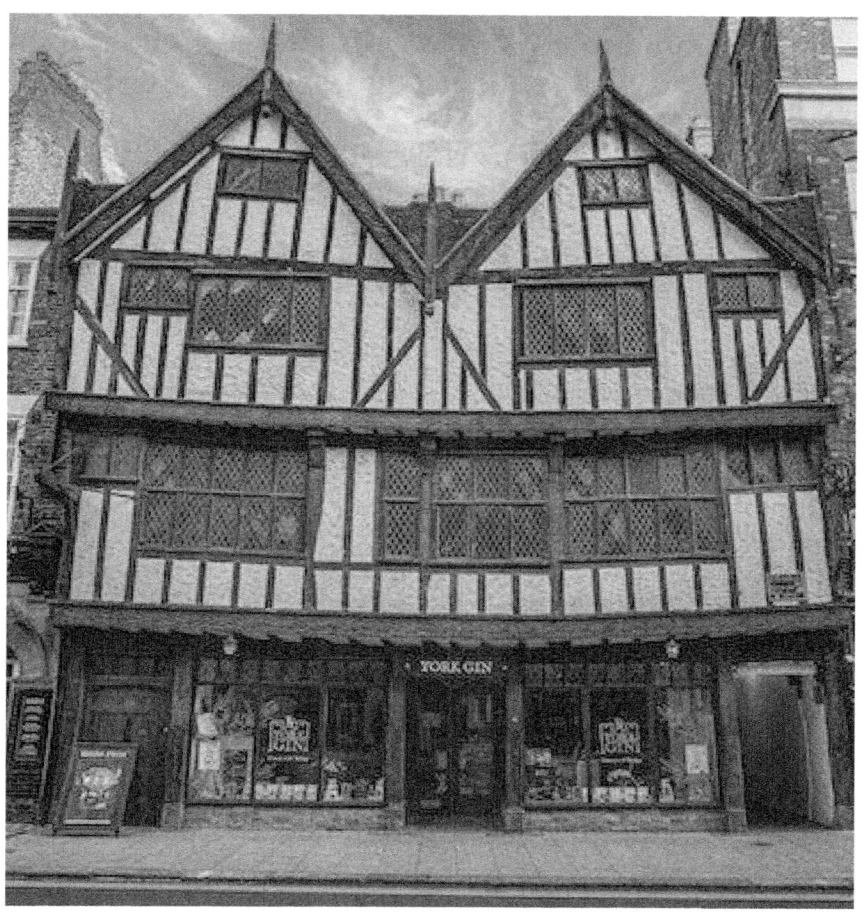

Chapter 8: Hidden Gems and Local Secrets

Beyond the well-trodden paths and popular attractions, York harbors a collection of hidden gems and local secrets that offer a more intimate and unique experience of the city. These lesser-known treasures provide a chance to connect with the local culture, history, and charm specially. Here are some hidden gems waiting to be discovered:

8.1 York's Snickelways: Hidden Medieval Paths

Beneath the surface of York's bustling streets lies a network of narrow, twisting alleyways known as "snickelways." These charming and evocative passages offer a glimpse into York's medieval past, transporting you back in time and providing a unique perspective on the city's history and architecture. As you traverse these hidden gems, you'll uncover the stories and secrets that have shaped York's character over the centuries.

"Snickelway" is a term coined by local author Mark W. Jones, combining "snicket" (a northern English word for a narrow passageway) and "alleyway." Snickelways are often narrow, cobbled paths that wind their way through York's historic core, connecting streets, squares, and landmarks. Walking through snickelways feels like stepping into a time capsule, as these paths have retained much of their medieval charm and character. Along these passages, you'll encounter hidden courtyards, charming courtyards, quaint shops, and unexpected viewpoints.

- **Coffee Yard:** Coffee Yard is one of York's most iconic snickelways, characterized by its narrowness and historic architecture. Stroll down Coffee Yard to admire the timber-framed buildings and immerse yourself in its historic ambiance.
- **Goodramgate:** Goodramgate is both a main street and a snickelway, showcasing the blending of practicality and history in York. Explore the charming shops, boutiques, and traditional tea rooms that line Goodramgate.
- **Mad Alice Lane:** Mad Alice Lane is named after a local woman who was executed for murder in the 19th century. As you walk through Mad Alice Lane, consider the intriguing history and atmosphere that surrounds this narrow passage.
- **College Street:** College Street connects York Minster with St. William's College, a medieval building that once housed clergy. Enjoy the academic aura of the surroundings, as College Street is a reminder of York's ecclesiastical history.

- **The Hole in the Wall:** The Hole in the Wall is aptly named due to the passage passing through a small archway in the city wall. Traverse this passage to discover a cozy café and unique shops, tucked away in an unexpected location.
- **Poppleton Gate:** Poppleton Gate provides a break from the city's bustle, with its charming village-like atmosphere. Explore the snickelway's quieter ambiance and admire the quaint cottages and gardens along the route.
- **Ogleforth:** Ogleforth offers a tranquil escape from the city center's activity, providing a peaceful walkway. Enjoy glimpses of hidden gardens and charming residential areas as you stroll through Ogleforth.

8.2 York's Cat Trail: Feline-Inspired Exploration

Venture beyond the ordinary and embark on a playful and whimsical adventure through York by following the city's unique Cat Trail. This self-guided tour takes you on a journey to discover a collection of cat statues and sculptures scattered throughout York's charming streets. As you follow the trail, you'll uncover delightful feline-inspired surprises and enjoy a lighthearted perspective on the city's landmarks and attractions.

- **Concept:** The Cat Trail is a trail of cat statues and sculptures that are strategically placed in surprising and unexpected locations throughout York. The trail was initiated by local artists and enthusiasts to add a touch of fun and curiosity to the city's streets.
- **Exploring the Cat Trail:** The Cat Trail is a self-guided tour, allowing you to explore at your own pace and follow your route. Use a map or a guidebook to locate the cat statues and discover their unique placements.
- **York's Quirky Cat Statues:** Each cat statue has its distinctive design, expression, and placement, adding to the charm and intrigue of the trail. You'll find cats on windowsills, rooftops, doorways, and even perched atop historical landmarks.
- **Cat-Themed Landmarks:** Some cats may sport colorful yarn wraps, adding an artistic and playful touch to their appearance. The cat statues are often placed near York's popular attractions and landmarks, creating a unique fusion of feline charm and historical significance.
- **Engagement and Discovery:** The Cat Trail is ideal for families with children, as it offers an engaging and enjoyable way to explore the city. The trail encourages interaction and curiosity, making it a memorable experience for visitors of all ages.
- **Cat Trail Souvenirs:** Look for cat-themed souvenirs and mementos inspired by the trail,

such as postcards, magnets, and cat-related merchandise. These souvenirs allow you to take a piece of the Cat Trail's charm with you as a reminder of your whimsical adventure.
- **Connecting with the Community:** The Cat Trail has become a beloved part of York's community, with locals and visitors alike participating in the joy of discovery. Engaging in the Cat Trail connects you with fellow travelers and locals who share a passion for whimsy and exploration.
- **Adding Playfulness to Exploration:** The Cat Trail offers a unique way to explore York's historic streets while adding an element of playfulness and surprise to your journey. Keep your eyes peeled for cats in unexpected places, and enjoy the thrill of discovering each whimsical sculpture.
- **Kitty-Approved Adventur**e: The Cat Trail invites you to see York from a new perspective, where historical landmarks are paired with playful cats. Capture memorable photos with the cat statues, creating lasting memories of your kitty-approved adventure.

8.3 Ghost Walks and Haunted York

Step into the shadows and uncover the spine-chilling tales that have woven a tapestry of ghostly history throughout York. Known for its rich history and ancient architecture, York holds a darker side filled with stories of restless spirits, haunted buildings, and eerie occurrences. Join one of the city's ghost walks to explore the haunted corners and unearth the mysteries that linger in the depths of its past.

1. **York's Haunting Legacy:** York's long history contributes to its reputation as one of the most haunted cities in England, with centuries of stories and legends. The city's ancient buildings, narrow alleyways, and cobbled streets provide the perfect backdrop for ghostly tales.
2. **Ghost Walks and Tours:** York offers a variety of ghost walks and tours, each with its unique focus, style, and atmosphere. Professional guides lead the way, sharing eerie stories and tales of the supernatural as you explore the city's darker corners.
3. **Haunted Locations:** One of York's most haunted pubs, the Golden Fleece Inn, is said to be home to several restless spirits. The historic street of The Shambles is known for its charming architecture and also its tales of hauntings and paranormal encounters.
4. **The Ghost of Roman Legionnaires:** According to legend, the ghostly apparitions of Roman legionnaires have been spotted walking along the ancient Roman roads in York. Some claim to have encountered these spectral soldiers while walking through the city's historic streets.

5. **The Ghost of the Grey Lady:** The Grey Lady, believed to be the spirit of a former actress, is said to haunt the York Theatre Royal. Theatre staff and actors have reported feeling her presence and experiencing unexplained phenomena.
6. **Haunted York Minster:** York Minster, a grand and historic cathedral, is rumored to be haunted by various ghosts, including the figure of a Roman soldier. Join a ghost walk to hear the eerie stories surrounding York Minster and its spectral inhabitants.
7. **The Haunted Treasurers' House:** This historic mansion is rumored to be haunted by Roman soldiers marching through its cellars. Visitors have reported experiencing strange phenomena, including "time slips" where they feel transported to the past.
8. **Atmospheric Nighttime Tours:** Many ghost walks and tours take place after dark, enhancing the eerie atmosphere and adding a layer of spookiness. Wander through York's historic streets with lantern-lit tours that bring an authentic touch to the ghostly experience.

Tips for Ghost Walks

- **Dress Comfortably:** Wear comfortable clothing and footwear, as ghost walks often involve walking through uneven terrain and atmospheric settings.

- **Open Mind:** Keep an open mind and immerse yourself in the stories and atmosphere, even if you're skeptical about the supernatural.
- **Capture Memories:** Bring a camera or smartphone to capture the atmosphere and locations of the stories you encounter.
- **Respectful Attitude:** Remember that ghost walks are not only about scares but also about storytelling and the city's history, so approach the experience with respect.

8.4 Homestead Park: A Local Favorite

Nestled within the heart of York, Homestead Park stands as a serene oasis cherished by both locals and visitors seeking a peaceful escape from the city's hustle and bustle. This beautifully landscaped park offers a harmonious blend of natural beauty, recreational spaces, and a touch of history, making it a cherished haven for relaxation and leisure.

1. **Overview of Homestead Park:** Homestead Park was originally part of the estate of Terry's chocolate factory, adding a touch of historical significance to its landscape. The park was transformed from private gardens into a public space, preserving its elegance while opening its gates to the community.
2. **Natural Beauty and Landscaping:** The park's well-maintained greenery, flowerbeds,

and tree-lined paths create a tranquil environment that invites visitors to unwind. Enjoy the peaceful atmosphere as you stroll around the park's ponds, watching ducks and other waterfowl.

3. **Relaxation and Leisure:** Homestead Park offers ample open spaces where visitors can relax, have picnics, read a book, or simply bask in the sun. Families with children can make use of the play area, complete with swings and other recreational facilities.
4. **Community Garden:** The park features a community garden known as the Green Fingers Project, where volunteers cultivate flowers and vegetables. Visitors are encouraged to participate in the garden's activities and even try their hand at gardening.
5. **Events and Activities:** Homestead Park hosts various workshops, events, and outdoor activities that cater to different interests and age groups. Look out for special outdoor theatre performances that take advantage of the park's inviting atmosphere.
6. **Terry's Clock Tower:** The clock tower, an iconic remnant of Terry's chocolate factory, adds a touch of history and charm to the park. The tower serves as a memorial to those who worked at the factory and adds a unique element to the park's ambiance.
7. **Sensory Garden:** The sensory garden is designed to engage all five senses, offering a truly immersive experience for visitors. Explore

plants with unique textures and fragrances, making the garden a sensory delight.
8. **Riverside Walks:** Homestead Park's location along the River Ouse offers visitors the opportunity for peaceful riverside walks. Take in picturesque views of the river and surrounding areas as you meander along the paths.
9. **Local Connection:** Homestead Park is a beloved spot for York's residents, providing a tranquil retreat just a stone's throw away from the city center. The park often hosts local community events and gatherings, fostering a sense of togetherness.
10. **Enjoying the Simple Pleasures:** Pack a picnic and find a shaded spot to enjoy a leisurely meal amidst the park's natural beauty. Bring a book and find a cozy reading nook, letting the soothing environment enhance your reading experience.
11. **Capturing the Moment:** Capture the park's beauty through photography, whether it's the vibrant flowers, serene ponds, or the historic clock tower. Take a moment to pause, breathe, and appreciate the calm atmosphere that Homestead Park offers.

8.5 Off-the-Beaten-Path Museums

Beyond the well-known museums that adorn York's streets, hidden gems are waiting to be discovered by those with a penchant for unique and niche cultural experiences. These off-the-beaten-path museums offer a different perspective on history, art, and curiosity, taking you on a journey of discovery that sets them apart from mainstream attractions. Delve into these lesser-known museums for a truly enriching and memorable exploration of York's diverse heritage.

1. **York Castle Museum:** York Castle Museum is famous for its recreated historical street "Kirkgate," which transports you back in time. Explore a range of exhibits, including social history, fashion, toys, and more, providing insights into everyday life throughout history.
2. **Richard III Experience at Monk Bar:** Situated within Monk Bar, this exhibit offers a glimpse into the life and reign of King Richard III. Engage with the history and legend of Richard III through interactive displays and informative exhibits.
3. **National Centre for Early Music:** Housed in a medieval church, this center celebrates early music through concerts, workshops, and exhibits. Attend live performances of historical music and take part in workshops that delve into the world of early musical traditions.

4. **Quilt Museum and Gallery:** Tucked away in an unassuming building, this museum showcases the art and history of quilting. Admire intricate quilts that showcase craftsmanship and creativity across different periods and cultures.
5. **Bar Convent Living Heritage Centre:** Learn about the Bar Convent's history and its significance to Catholic heritage. It is the oldest active convent in England. Take guided tours to learn about the convent's history, its role in education, and its connections to notable historical figures.
6. **York Cold War Bunker:** Explore an underground bunker that was once a top-secret nuclear monitoring post during the Cold War. Delve into the tense history of the Cold War era as you explore the bunker's rooms and equipment.
7. **The York Dungeon:** The York Dungeon offers a theatrical and interactive experience that brings dark historical tales to life. Through humor and drama, learn about the city's darker history, from the Plague to the Gunpowder Plot.
8. **Barley Hall:** Barley Hall is a meticulously restored medieval townhouse that offers an immersive journey into the past. Experience the lifestyle of a prosperous merchant family as you explore the halls, chambers, and artifacts of the medieval era.
9. **The York Army Museum:** The York Army Museum delves into the history of the British

Army and its connections to York. Discover artifacts, uniforms, and exhibits that provide insights into the life of soldiers and their contributions to history.
10. **The Henry VII Experience:** Step back into the Tudor era and explore the life and reign of King Henry VII at Micklegate Bar. Learn about the political and social context of Henry VII's reign through interactive exhibits.

8.6 Meeting Locals: Cultural Exchange

While exploring the attractions and landmarks of York is a must, engaging with the local community offers a deeper and more meaningful connection to the city's culture and way of life. Embarking on a cultural exchange with the residents of York allows you to gain insights, make new friends, and experience the city from a unique perspective. Here are some ways to immerse yourself in the local culture and foster memorable interactions with York's welcoming community.

1. **Attend Local Events and Festivals:** York hosts a variety of events and festivals throughout the year, celebrating everything from food and music to history and arts. Participate in these events, mingle with locals, and join in the festivities to experience York's vibrant community spirit.

2. **Visit Local Markets:** Engage with local artisans, producers, and traders at Shambles Market, where you can discover handmade crafts, fresh produce, and local delicacies. Explore Newgate Market for a taste of local flavors and a chance to interact with traders who have been a part of York's market tradition.
3. **Join Workshops and Classes:** Take part in craft workshops, cooking classes, or artistic sessions hosted by local artisans and experts. Engage in a cultural exchange by sharing your skills and knowledge while learning from locals in a friendly and collaborative setting.
4. **Attend Local Performances:** Attend performances at local theaters, music venues, and pubs to enjoy live entertainment and engage with the artistic community. Strike up conversations with fellow attendees and performers to gain insights into York's arts and entertainment scene.
5. **Explore Neighbourhoods:** Venture into residential neighborhoods to experience the everyday life of locals away from the tourist hotspots. Visit local cafés and pubs, and strike up conversations with patrons and staff to learn more about the local lifestyle.
6. **Engage in Volunteer Activities:** Participate in volunteer programs or community activities that align with your interests, contributing positively to the city's well-being. Collaborating on projects with locals allows you to build

meaningful connections while making a difference.
7. **Attend Talks and Lectures:** Attend talks, lectures, and discussions hosted by local organizations, covering topics ranging from history and culture to contemporary issues. Engage in conversations with both speakers and attendees to share perspectives and insights.
8. **Support Local Businesses:** Visit independent shops, boutiques, and eateries, where you can interact with local entrepreneurs and learn about their passion for their businesses. Ask for recommendations from shop owners and employees to discover hidden gems and local favorites.
9. **Participate in Sports and Activities:** Join local sports clubs or fitness groups to bond over shared activities and enjoy recreational pursuits with local enthusiasts. Engage in friendly competition, play matches, and engage in post-game conversations with fellow participants.
10. **Engage on Social Media:** Connect with York's community through social media platforms and local forums to stay informed about events, activities, and discussions. Engage in online conversations to ask questions, seek recommendations, and connect with locals before your visit.

Chapter 9: Shopping and Souvenirs

Exploring York's vibrant streets isn't just about sightseeing—it's also a chance to discover unique treasures that you can carry with you to remember your visit. From charming boutiques to bustling markets, York offers a plethora of shopping options where you can find souvenirs, local products, and distinctive gifts that reflect the city's character and heritage.

9.1 Coney Street and High Petergate:

Coney Street and High Petergate are two of York's bustling shopping districts that offer a diverse range of shops, boutiques, and eateries. These vibrant streets are perfect for both strolls and dedicated shopping sprees, allowing you to discover a variety of products, from high-street fashion to unique local finds. Immerse yourself in the energy of these districts as you explore the array of options they have to offer.

Coney Street: Retail Haven on the River

- **High-Street Fashion:** Coney Street is home to popular high-street fashion retailers, making it a go-to destination for clothing, shoes, and accessories.
- **Variety:** You'll find a mix of well-known chains and established brands, catering to different styles and preferences.
- **Local Flavors:** Amid the larger stores, keep an eye out for independent boutiques and local shops offering unique and handcrafted items.
- **Eateries:** Alongside the shopping, Coney Street hosts various cafes and restaurants, providing a convenient spot for refreshments and meals.
- **River Views:** Enjoy the pleasant views of the River Ouse as you explore Coney Street, adding an extra layer of charm to your shopping experience.

High Petergate: Heritage and Shopping Blend

- **Historic Charm:** High Petergate runs from Bootham Bar to York Minster, offering a blend of historic architecture and contemporary shops.
- **Boutiques and Galleries:** Wander through this street to discover boutiques, galleries, and

shops offering art, fashion, jewelry, and antiques.
- **Cultural Stops:** High Petergate is also home to cultural sites such as York Minster and the Treasurer's House, adding a touch of heritage to your visit.
- **Cafes and Pubs:** Take a break from shopping by visiting the street's cafes, tearooms, and traditional pubs, providing a cozy atmosphere to relax in.
- **Local Crafts:** Seek out independent stores that showcase local craftsmanship, allowing you to find unique souvenirs and gifts with a personal touch.

Exploring the Blend

Both Coney Street and High Petergate offer a balance between shopping and cultural exploration, allowing you to seamlessly transition from perusing boutiques to visiting historical sites. The districts are conveniently located near York's major attractions, making them ideal for those looking to combine shopping with sightseeing. As you stroll down these bustling streets, take in the vibrant atmosphere, interact with locals, and uncover the treasures that these districts have to offer. Whether you're seeking fashionable finds, local crafts, or simply a charming atmosphere, Coney Street and High Petergate are sure to provide a satisfying shopping and cultural experience in the heart of York.

In addition to the streets, Here are some great places to go shopping and souvenir hunting in York:

- **The Shambles:** It is a historic street in York that is lined with timber-framed buildings. It is a popular tourist destination and a great place to find souvenirs, gifts, and antiques.
- **Stonegate:** Stonegate is another historic street in York that is home to a mix of stores hidden amongst medieval and Georgian architecture. It is a great place to find independent shops and boutiques.
- **The Minster Market**: This is a street market that is held every Wednesday and Saturday in the shadow of York Minster. It is a great place to find fresh produce, meats, cheeses, and other local products.
- **Bettys**: This is a chain of tea rooms that is known for its traditional afternoon tea. They also have several stores that sell souvenirs, gifts, and food items.
- **The Yorkshire Museum:** It has a gift shop that sells a variety of souvenirs, gifts, and books related to Yorkshire history and culture.

9.2 Unique Souvenirs from York

When it comes to selecting souvenirs from York, consider choosing items that encapsulate the city's rich history, culture, and local craftsmanship. These unique mementos not only serve as reminders of your visit but also offer a piece of York's charm to take home with you. Here are some distinctive souvenirs that capture the essence of York:

1. *York Minster Inspired Items*
- **Jewelry:** Look for jewelry inspired by the intricate designs of York Minster's stained glass windows and architectural details.
- **Ornaments:** Pick up decorative ornaments featuring York Minster's iconic silhouette or its intricate stone carvings.
- **Books:** Explore the cathedral's history through beautifully illustrated books that delve into its architecture, art, and significance.

2. *Yorkshire Tea and Tea Accessories*
- **Yorkshire Tea:** Take home a box of Yorkshire Tea, a renowned local brand that represents the city's tea-drinking culture.
- **Tea Accessories:** Consider purchasing a tea infuser, teapot, or tea towel featuring York-related designs.

3. *York's Chocolate Treats*
- **Chocolate Boxes:** Indulge in a variety of chocolate treats and confections from York's historic chocolate shops.
- **Chocolate Bars:** Choose artisanal chocolate bars inspired by York's chocolate-making heritage, with unique flavors and ingredients.

4. ***Quirky Cat-Themed Souvenirs***
   - **Cat Memorabilia:** As a nod to York's famous Cat Trail, find cat-themed merchandise, from keychains to clothing.
   - **Art Prints:** Look for art prints or illustrations featuring playful depictions of cats in iconic York settings.
5. ***Viking-Inspired Items***
   - **Viking Jewelry:** Discover pieces of jewelry inspired by York's Viking history, such as Thor's hammer pendants or Norse-inspired rings.
   - **Viking Souvenirs:** Explore Viking-themed souvenirs like drinking horns, shields, and figurines.
6. ***Handmade Crafts and Artwork***
   - **Local Artisan Crafts:** Seek out local artisans' shops for handmade pottery, textiles, woodwork, and glassware.
   - **Paintings and Prints:** Purchase artwork that captures York's landmarks, streets, and landscapes in unique and creative ways.
7. ***Historic Maps and Postcards***
   - **Antique Maps:** Acquire vintage-style maps of York that showcase its historical layout and landmarks.
   - **Postcards:** Collect postcards featuring York's famous sights or artistic representations to send to loved ones or keep as mementos.
8. ***Historical Books and Literature***
   - **Literary Connections:** Choose books set in or inspired by York, such as historical novels, travel guides, or local poetry collections.

- **Local Authors:** Look for works by local authors that offer insights into York's history, culture, and stories.

9. *Culinary Delicacies*
- **Yorkshire Produce:** Sample and purchase regional products like Yorkshire cheeses, chutneys, biscuits, and traditional ales.
- **Gift Baskets:** Create custom gift baskets with an assortment of local culinary treats to savor after your trip.

10. *Museum and Gallery Merchandise*
- **Art Gallery Prints:** Select prints of artworks from York's art galleries, allowing you to bring a piece of the city's art scene home.
- **Museum Merchandise:** Visit museum shops for merchandise related to their exhibits, including historical replicas and educational items.

Personalized Keepsakes

Choosing unique souvenirs from York is a way to bring the city's essence into your everyday life. Each item you select carries a story, reflecting the history, culture, and experiences that York has to offer. Whether you're drawn to historical landmarks, artistic creations, or the flavors of the region, these souvenirs will remind you of the moments you spent immersing yourself in York's captivating atmosphere.

9.3 Practical Shopping Tips

Navigating the shopping scene in York can be a delightful and rewarding experience. To make the most of your shopping adventure, consider these practical tips that will help you find the best deals, discover unique items, and enjoy a stress-free shopping experience in the city.

1. **Plan Your Shopping Route:** Before setting out, create a rough plan of the areas and shops you want to visit. This will help you make efficient use of your time and ensure you don't miss out on any must-see boutiques or markets.
2. **Comfortable Shoes:** York's streets are charming but can be quite uneven. Wear comfortable walking shoes that will allow you to explore the city's shopping districts without discomfort.
3. **Local Markets and Events:** Keep an eye out for local markets and events happening during your visit. These are excellent opportunities to discover unique items and engage with local artisans.
4. **Timing Matters:** Visit popular shopping areas early in the day to avoid crowds. Weekdays are generally less crowded than weekends, and mornings are often quieter than afternoons.
5. **Be Open to Discoveries:** While having a shopping list is helpful, be open to discovering unexpected treasures. York's boutiques and

markets offer a wide variety of items, and you might find something truly special when you least expect it.
6. **Support Local:** Choose to shop at locally owned stores and boutiques. This not only supports the local economy but also gives you a chance to discover unique items that may not be available in larger chain stores.
7. **Engage with Shopkeepers:** Shopkeepers often have valuable insights about their products and the local area. Strike up conversations, ask questions, and seek their recommendations—it can lead you to hidden gems.
8. **Bargaining and Negotiating:** While bargaining isn't common in most shops in York, it's worth asking if there's any flexibility on prices, especially if you're purchasing multiple items.
9. **Quality Over Quantity:** Focus on finding high-quality items that truly resonate with you, rather than buying a large quantity of souvenirs. Quality items will bring more joy and lasting memories.
10. **Check Return Policies:** Before making a purchase, especially for clothing or accessories, familiarize yourself with the store's return and exchange policies to avoid any inconvenience later.
11. **Keep an Eye on Local Discounts:** Look out for local discounts, loyalty programs, or student

discounts if applicable. Some stores may offer special deals for tourists as well.
12. **Carry a Reusable Bag:** Help reduce plastic waste by carrying a reusable bag with you. Many stores and markets in York support sustainability by minimizing plastic usage.
13. **Payment Options:** Ensure you have a mix of payment options, including cash and cards, as not all places may accept all forms of payment.
14. **Stay Hydrated and Take Breaks:** Shopping can be tiring, so remember to stay hydrated and take breaks to rest and enjoy the local cafes and eateries.
15. **Enjoy the Experience:** Shopping in York is not just about acquiring items—it's about immersing yourself in the city's culture, meeting local artisans, and creating memories. Take your time and enjoy the moment.

Remember, shopping in York is a chance to engage with the city's character, explore its diverse offerings, and bring home a piece of its charm. Whether you're seeking fashion, antiques, handmade crafts, or souvenirs, these practical tips will help you navigate the shopping scene with ease and enjoyment.

Chapter 10: Nightlife and Entertainment

10.1 Late-Night Activities

York offers a variety of late-night activities that cater to different interests, from historical explorations to vibrant social scenes. Here are some great ways to enjoy York after dark:

1. **Ghost Walks and Tours:** York is famous for its haunted history and ghost stories, making ghost walks one of the most popular late-night activities. You can join guided tours that take you through the city's narrow medieval streets and hidden corners, where you'll hear chilling tales of ghosts, mysterious events, and historical hauntings. Popular options include The Original Ghost Walk of York and The Bloody Tour of York.
2. **Evening Stroll along The Shambles:** One of the most picturesque streets in the UK, The Shambles, is especially atmospheric at night. Wander through the narrow, cobbled streets with medieval overhanging timber-framed buildings. The area is beautifully illuminated in the evening, providing a peaceful late-night walk with fewer tourists around.
3. **Late-Night Dining:** York's restaurant scene offers plenty of late-night dining options, from

cozy pubs serving hearty meals to upscale restaurants offering fine dining experiences. For something casual, you can try Evil Eye or The House of Trembling Madness, which offer both great food and an impressive selection of drinks. For a more refined experience, restaurants like Skosh or The Star Inn The City provide late-night fine dining.

4. **Pub Culture and Craft Beer:** York is home to a number of historic and atmospheric pubs, many of which stay open late. Some favorites include Ye Olde Starre Inne, York's oldest pub, and The Golden Fleece, which is reputedly haunted. York also has a strong craft beer scene, and places like Brew York and The Fossgate Social are popular with locals and visitors alike.
5. **York Minster by Night:** York Minster occasionally hosts special events like candlelit services or evening concerts. Even if there's no event, the Minster is beautifully lit up at night, and a nighttime visit to the square surrounding this iconic cathedral is a peaceful and stunning experience.
6. **Cinema and Theater:** For late-night entertainment, York's City Screen Picturehouse offers regular screenings of new releases, independent films, and cult classics. Alternatively, you can catch an evening performance at The York Theatre Royal or The Grand Opera House, both of which host plays, musicals, and comedy shows.

7. **Late-Night Shopping and Cafés:** Some of York's independent shops stay open later on certain nights, especially during festivals or seasonal events. If you're into books, The Minster Gate Bookshop is a charming place to visit. For a late-night coffee, head to Bison Coffee House or Brew & Brownie, which offer great coffee and a relaxed vibe.
8. **Nightlife in Micklegate:** If you're looking for a lively night out, head to Micklegate, which is known for its bars, pubs, and clubs. Popular spots like The Drawing Board and The Micklegate Social stay open late and are known for their cocktails and energetic atmospheres. Clubs like Kuda or Flares provide options for dancing and late-night fun.
9. **River Ouse Night Cruise:** York offers evening river cruises along the River Ouse. These night cruises provide a relaxed way to see the city illuminated at night, with the historic architecture reflecting in the water. Some cruises even offer drinks and live entertainment on board.
10. **Escape Rooms:** For a fun group activity, try one of York's escape rooms, many of which offer evening sessions. Places like Mindlock Escape Rooms and Can You Escape? York provide themed challenges where you and your friends can solve puzzles to "escape" within a set time.

With a mix of history, culture, and social activities, York comes alive at night, providing plenty of options for entertainment and exploration after the sun goes down.

10.2 Bars and Pubs

York is famous for its vibrant pub culture, boasting a mix of historic and contemporary bars. Here are some of the best bars and pubs to check out for a memorable night out:

1. **The Golden Fleece:** The Golden Fleece claims to be the most haunted pub in York, with a history dating back over 500 years. This atmospheric pub features low ceilings, wooden beams, and a collection of historical artifacts that transport you back in time. Join a ghost tour and hear about the pub's ghostly inhabitants while enjoying a drink in its old-world setting.
2. **The Guy Fawkes Inn:** Named after the infamous Guy Fawkes, this inn is believed to have been his birthplace. With its timbered façade and period details, the inn captures the essence of York's medieval heritage. Enjoy a drink in the traditional pub or consider staying overnight in one of its historic rooms.
3. **The Maltings:** The Maltings is known for its extensive selection of real ales, ciders, and craft beers. Its snug and cozy interior provides the perfect environment for sampling local brews. The staff's expertise in ales ensures you'll find the perfect drink to suit your taste.

4. **The House of the Trembling Madness:** This pub combines a traditional pub setting with a medieval-themed shop offering unique drinks and merchandise. The House of the Trembling Madness boasts an impressive selection of craft beers and ales. Decorated with curiosities and oddities, the pub's ambiance adds to its distinctive charm.
5. **The Eagle & Child:** It is a popular pub with a traditional British atmosphere. The pub serves a wide selection of beers and ciders, as well as pub food. The Eagle & Child is also a great place to watch live sports.
6. **The Chopping Block at Walmgate Ale House:** This is a bistro-style pub with a focus on seasonal food. The menu features dishes such as steak frites, fish and chips, and moules frites. The pub also has a wide selection of beers and wines.
7. **Brew York:** Brew York is a brewery with a taproom and beer garden. The taproom has 12 beers on tap, as well as a selection of guest beers. The beer garden is a great place to enjoy a pint of beer on a sunny day.
8. **The Hop:** This is a pub with a two-level interior. The first level has a traditional pub atmosphere, while the second level has a more modern vibe. The Hop serves a wide selection of beers, wines, and cocktails.
9. **The Fossgate Social:** This is a gastropub with a focus on locally-sourced food. The menu features dishes such as lamb shank, fish and

chips, and steak frites. The Fossgate Social also has a wide selection of beers and wines.
10. **The Walmgate Ale House:** This is a traditional pub with a focus on real ales. The pub has over 10 beers on tap, as well as a selection of bottled beers. The Walmgate Ale House is also a great place to try local Yorkshire beers.

York's pubs and bars offer everything from historic charm to modern, trendy experiences. Whether you're after traditional ales, craft beers, cocktails, or a haunting story, there's a place in York's nightlife scene for everyone.

10.3 Nightclubs

York may be more famous for its historic pubs, but the city also offers a few great options for those looking to dance the night away. Here are some of the top nightclubs in York for a lively night out:

Central and City Centre

1. **The Basement:** Known for its eclectic mix of music and events, The Basement is a popular choice for students and locals alike. It's a multi-room venue with a variety of spaces to explore, from the main dancefloor to quieter areas for chatting.
2. **The Fulford Arms:** This traditional pub with a modern twist offers live music, DJ sets, and a

lively atmosphere. With its exposed brick walls and wooden beams, The Fulford Arms has a classic British pub feel, but it also hosts regular events and live music.
3. **The House of Trembling Trees:** A quirky and alternative venue with a focus on indie music and underground events. It's a smaller, more intimate space with a unique atmosphere.
4. **The Stone Roses:** A popular student bar with a relaxed atmosphere and a range of events. It's a great place to grab a drink, play pool, and enjoy live music.

Student-Centric Venues

1. **The Duchess:** A classic student bar with a relaxed vibe and regular events. It's a popular spot for students to meet up and enjoy live music and sports screenings.
2. **The Priory:** A large, multi-room venue with a variety of music and events, catering to students and young professionals. It's a great place to dance the night away or enjoy a quieter atmosphere in one of its smaller rooms.
3. **The Eye Cue:** A popular student bar with a relaxed atmosphere and regular events. It's a great place to grab a drink, play pool, and enjoy live music.

Alternative and Indie Venues

1. **The Fibbers:** A legendary music venue showcasing local and international bands. It's a

must-visit for music lovers, with a diverse lineup of genres and a passionate crowd.
2. **The Crescent:** A popular venue for alternative and indie music, with a focus on emerging artists. It's a smaller, more intimate space with a dedicated following of music fans.
3. **The Stables:** A historic venue with a diverse range of music and events, from rock to jazz. It's a larger venue with a more formal atmosphere, perfect for those looking for a night out with a bit of history.

For a Night Out with a View

1. **The Roof Terrace at The Principal York:** Enjoy panoramic views of the city while sipping cocktails and dancing at this rooftop bar. It's a great spot for a special night out or to celebrate a special occasion.
2. **The Terrace at The Assembly**: Another rooftop bar with stunning views and a lively atmosphere. It's a popular spot for people-watching and enjoying the summer weather.

The nightlife scene in York can be dynamic, with new venues opening and closing regularly. It's always a good idea to check online reviews and social media pages for the latest updates. Whether you're into retro hits, indie rock, or house music, York's nightclubs offer a range of vibes and music styles to suit different tastes.

Chapter 11: Accommodation Options

York offers a variety of accommodation options that cater to different preferences and budgets, all within the backdrop of its historic charm. Whether you're seeking a luxurious stay, a cozy inn, or a budget-friendly hostel, you'll find the perfect place to rest and rejuvenate. Here's a selection of accommodation choices in York:

11.1 Luxury Hotels

For travelers seeking indulgence and a lavish experience, York boasts a selection of high-end luxury hotels and resorts. These properties often offer exclusive amenities. Here are 10 of the best luxury hotels in York, their price, and amenities:

1. **The Grand, York:** Price Starting at £250 per night, 5-star hotel with a spa, a gym, and a rooftop terrace with views of York Minster.
2. **No.1 by GuestHouse, York:** Price Starting at £175 per night, 4-star hotel with a spa, a gym, and a rooftop terrace with views of the city.
3. **Malmaison York:** Price Starting at £190 per night, 4-star hotel with a spa, a gym, and a bar with live music.

4. **Middlethorpe Hall & Spa:** Price Starting at £300 per night, 5-star hotel with a spa, a golf course, and a tennis court.
5. **Dean Court York:** Price Starting at £200 per night, 4-star hotel with a spa, a gym, and a restaurant with a Michelin star.
6. **Hilton York:** Price Starting at £150 per night, 4-star hotel with a gym, a bar, and a restaurant.
7. **Principal York:** Price Starting at £180 per night, 4-star hotel with a spa, a gym, and a restaurant.
8. **York Marriott Hotel & Spa:** Price Starting at £200 per night, 4-star hotel with a spa, a gym, and a restaurant.
9. **Judges Court Hotel:** Price Starting at £180 per night. This hotel has a spa, a gym, and a restaurant
10. **Ramada York:** Price Starting at £120 per night, 3-star hotel with a gym, a bar, and a restaurant.

11.2 Boutique and Mid-Range Hotels

Here are 10 of the best boutique and mid-range hotels in York, their price, and amenities:

1. **Little White Hotel York:** Price starting at £130 per night. A 4-star hotel with a bar, a restaurant, and a gym. It is located in a charming townhouse in the heart of York.

2. **Hotel Indigo York:** The price starts at £150 per night. A 4-star hotel with a bar, a restaurant, and a gym. It is located in a modern building with a rooftop terrace with city views.
3. **York House Hotel:** The price starts at £120 per night. A 4-star hotel with a bar, a restaurant, and a gym. It is located in a Georgian townhouse with a garden.
4. **The Principal York:** Price starting at £180 per night. A 4-star hotel with a spa, a gym, and a restaurant. It is located in a historic building in the heart of York.
5. **Chambers Hotel York:** Price starting at £140 per night. A 4-star hotel with a bar, a restaurant, and a gym. It is located in a modern building with a rooftop terrace with city views.
6. **Grays Court Hotel:** Price starting at £160 per night. A 4-star hotel with a spa, a gym, and a restaurant. It is located in a Georgian townhouse with a garden.
7. **York Walls Hotel:** Price starting at £100 per night. A 3-star hotel with a bar, a restaurant, and a gym. It is located in a historic building on the city walls.
8. **City Walls Guest House:** Price starting at £80 per night. A 3-star guest house with a bar, a restaurant, and a garden. It is located in a historic building on the city walls.
9. **York Backpackers:** Price starting at £35 per night. A hostel with a bar, a kitchen, and a shared room. It is located in a central location in York.

10. **YHA York:** Price starting at £40 per night. A hostel with a bar, a kitchen, and a shared room. It is located in a central location in York.

11.3 Guesthouses and B&Bs

Enjoy a warm and personalized experience at a bed and breakfast, where you can savor homemade breakfasts and immerse yourself in local hospitality. Here are 10 of the best guesthouses and B&Bs in York, their price, and amenities:

1. **The Bishopthorpe Arms:** Price starting at £100 per night. A 4-star guest house with a bar, a restaurant, and a garden. It is located in a historic building in the heart of York.
2. **The Old Curiosity Shop:** Price starting at £120 per night. A 3-star guest house with a bar, a restaurant, and a garden. It is located in a historic building in the heart of York.
3. **The Black Swan Inn:** Price starting at £100 per night. A 3-star guest house with a bar, a restaurant, and a garden. It is located on the banks of the River Ouse in York.
4. **The King's Arms:** Price starting at £80 per night. A 3-star guest house with a bar, a restaurant, and a garden. It is located in a historic building in the heart of York.
5. **The Grange Guest House:** The price starts at £70 per night. A 3-star guest house with a bar, a

restaurant, and a garden. It is located in a Georgian townhouse in York.
6. **154 The Shambles:** Price starting at £90 per night. A 3-star guest house with a bar, a restaurant, and a garden. It is located in a historic building on The Shambles in York.
7. **Bardsley House:** Price starting at £100 per night. A 3-star guest house with a bar, a restaurant, and a garden. It is located in a Georgian townhouse in York.
8. **The Little White Lodge:** Price starts at £80 per night. A 3-star guest house with a bar, a restaurant, and a garden. It is located in a charming townhouse in York.
9. **The York House Hotel:** The price starts at £120 per night. A 4-star guest house with a bar, a restaurant, and a gym. It is located in a Georgian townhouse with a garden.
10. **York Backpackers**: Price starting at £35 per night. A hostel with a bar, a kitchen, and a common room. It is located in a central location in York.

11.4 Self-Catering Apartments

For travelers who prefer more space and the convenience of a kitchen, self-catering apartments are available throughout the city. Here are 10 of the best self-catering apartments in York, their price, and amenities:

1. **Goodramgate Apartments:** Price starting at £100 per night. These apartments are located in a Georgian townhouse in the heart of York. They have fully equipped kitchens, private bathrooms, and free WiFi.
2. **The Apartments at Dean Court:** Price starting at £120 per night. These apartments are located in a 4-star hotel in York. They have fully equipped kitchens, private bathrooms, and a gym.
3. **York Central Apartments:** Price starting at £90 per night. These apartments are located in a modern building in the heart of York. They have fully equipped kitchens, private bathrooms, and a washing machine.
4. **The Shambles Apartments:** Price starting at £110 per night. These apartments are located in a historic building on The Shambles in York. They have fully equipped kitchens, private bathrooms, and a washing machine.
5. **The Monkgate Apartments:** Price starting at £80 per night. These apartments are located in a Georgian townhouse in York. They have fully equipped kitchens, private bathrooms, and a washing machine.
6. **The Apartments at Grays Court:** Prices start at £130 per night. These apartments are located in a 4-star hotel in York. They have fully equipped kitchens, private bathrooms, and a gym.
7. **YORK Central Apartments - Tower Street:** Price starting at £90 per night. These

apartments are located in a modern building in the heart of York. They have fully equipped kitchens, private bathrooms, and a washing machine.
8. **YORK Central Apartments - Blake Street:** Price starting at £90 per night. These apartments are located in a modern building in the heart of York. They have fully equipped kitchens, private bathrooms, and a washing machine.
9. **York Backpackers:** Price starting at £35 per night. This hostel has self-catering kitchenettes and shared bathrooms. It is located in a central location in York.
10. **The Lawrance Luxury Aparthotel - York:** Price starting at £150 per night. These chic apartments are situated in York on Mickelgate and Tanner Row. They have fully equipped kitchens, private bathrooms, and a gym.

11.5 Hostels and Budget Accommodation

here are 10 of the best hostels and budget accommodations in York, their price, and amenities:

1. **York Backpackers:** Price starting at £35 per night. This hostel has self-catering kitchenettes and shared bathrooms. It is located in a central location in York.

2. **YHA York:** Price starting at £40 per night. This hostel has self-catering kitchenettes and shared bathrooms. It is located in a central location in York.
3. **St. Christopher's Inn York:** Price starting at £45 per night. This hostel has dormitory rooms and private rooms. It is located in a central location in York.
4. **Safestay York:** Price starts at £50 per night. This hostel has dormitory rooms and private rooms. It is located in a central location in York.
5. **The YHA York Youth Hostel:** Price starts at £30 per night. This hostel has dormitory rooms and private rooms. It is located in a historic building in York.
6. **York Central Backpackers:** Price starting at £35 per night. This hostel has dormitory rooms and private rooms. It is located in a central location in York.
7. **York Bunkhouse:** Price starts at £30 per night. This hostel has dormitory rooms and private rooms. It is located in a central location in York.
8. **The Old Railway Station Hostel:** Price starting at £40 per night. This hostel has dormitory rooms and private rooms. It is located in a historic building in York.
9. **The York Minster Youth Hostel:** Price starts at £40 per night. This hostel has dormitory rooms and private rooms. It is located in a historic building in York.

10. **YHA Acomb:** Price starting at £35 per night. This hostel has dormitory rooms and private rooms. It is located in a peaceful location just outside of York.

11.6 Unique Stays

1. **The House of Trembling Madness:** Price starting at £195 per night | This quirky pub has rooms themed around different phobias, such as claustrophobia and arachnophobia. It is situated in York's center.
2. **The Golden Fleece:** Price starting at £150 per night | This historic inn has a haunted reputation and offers ghost-hunting tours. It is located in the heart of York.
3. **The Roman Bath House:** Price starting at £120 per night | This former bath house has been converted into a luxury hotel. It is situated in York's center.
4. **The Pig and Whistle:** Price starting at £100 per night | This traditional pub has rooms with four-poster beds and views of York Minster. It is located in the heart of York.
5. **The Shepherds Rest:** Price starting at £120 per night | This shepherd's hut is located in the countryside just outside of York. It has a hot tub and a wood-fired oven.
6. **The Boathouse:** Price starting at £150 per night | This boathouse is located on the River Ouse in York. It has a private deck and a hot tub.

7. **The Yurt:** Price starting at £100 per night | This yurt is located in the countryside just outside of York. It has a wood-burning stove and a barbecue.
8. **The Treehouse:** Price starting at £120 per night | This treehouse is located in the countryside just outside of York. It has a zip line and a swing.
9. **The Tipi:** Price starting at £100 per night | This tipi is located in the countryside just outside of York. It has a campfire and a telescope.
10. **The Cave:** Price starting at £150 per night | This cave is located in the countryside just outside of York. It has a hot tub and a waterfall.

Tips for Booking:

- **Location:** Consider your preferences for proximity to the city center, attractions, or a peaceful setting.
- **Reviews:** Check online reviews to gauge the experiences of previous guests and ensure the accommodation meets your expectations.
- **Booking in Advance:** Especially during peak tourist seasons, it's advisable to book your accommodation well in advance.
- **Amenities:** Decide on the amenities that matter most to you, whether it's free Wi-Fi, on-site dining, parking, or spa facilities.

Whether you're looking for a lavish stay, a cozy retreat, or a budget-friendly option, York's accommodation offerings are as diverse as its attractions. Whichever type of lodging you choose, you'll have the opportunity to fully immerse yourself in the city's historical ambiance and create lasting memories.

Chapter 12: Practical Information

12.1 Currency and Payment Options

Understanding the currency and payment options available in York will help you manage your finances smoothly during your visit. Here's what you need to know:

Currency: The currency used in the United Kingdom, including York, is the British Pound Sterling (GBP), often referred to simply as "pounds." It's important to familiarize yourself with the denominations of coins and banknotes:

- **Coins:** There are coins in various denominations, including 1p, 2p, 5p, 10p, 20p, 50p, £1, and £2.
- **Banknotes:** Banknotes come in different values, such as £5, £10, £20, and in some cases, £50. Note that Scottish and Northern Irish banknotes are also legal currency in the UK and can be used interchangeably.

Payment Options

- **Cash:** Carrying some cash is advisable for smaller purchases, transportation, and places

that might not accept cards. You can withdraw cash from ATMs (cash machines) located throughout the city. Major credit and debit cards are widely accepted, but having some cash on hand is always a good idea.
- **Credit and Debit Cards:** Credit and debit cards are commonly used in York for transactions. Visa and Mastercard are widely accepted, followed by American Express and other major card brands. Most shops, restaurants, hotels, and attractions accept card payments.
- **Contactless Payments:** Contactless payments, where you tap your card on a payment terminal, are widely accepted in York. This is especially convenient for small purchases like snacks, coffee, or quick souvenirs.
- **Mobile Payments:** Mobile payment options like Apple Pay and Google Pay are also becoming more prevalent in York. Make sure your device is set up for mobile payments before using this method.
- **Currency Exchange:** If you're carrying foreign currency, you can exchange it for British Pounds at banks, currency exchange offices, and some hotels. Keep in mind that exchange rates and fees may vary.
- **Tipping:** Tipping is customary in restaurants, cafes, and for services like taxis. A standard tip is around 10-15% of the total bill. Some

restaurants might include a service charge, so check the bill before adding a tip.
- **Payment Security:** When using your credit or debit card, always ensure that the payment terminal is secure and legitimate. Be cautious when providing card details over the phone or online.
- **Digital Banking Apps:** If you're comfortable with it, you can use mobile banking apps to manage your finances, check your account balance, and even make transfers while you're on the go.
- **Plan Ahead:** Before your trip, inform your bank or credit card company about your travel dates to avoid any potential issues with using your cards abroad. Some banks might block transactions from unfamiliar locations as a security measure.
- **Local Knowledge:** If you're unsure about payment options at a particular establishment, don't hesitate to ask the staff. They'll be happy to provide information about payment methods.

By being prepared with a mix of cash and cards, you'll be able to navigate York's payment landscape with ease, ensuring a hassle-free and enjoyable experience as you explore the city's attractions, shops, and dining options.

12.2 Packing Essentials and What to Wear

Packing for your trip to York requires a bit of preparation, especially considering the weather and the activities you'll be engaging in. Here's a guide to help you pack essentials and decide what to wear during your visit:

Weather Considerations

York's weather can be quite variable, so it's important to be prepared for different conditions:

- **Rain Gear:** Pack a compact umbrella and a waterproof jacket or raincoat. A foldable rain poncho can also be handy.
- **Layered Clothing:** Since the weather can change throughout the day, layering is key. Bring lightweight sweaters, cardigans, and long-sleeve shirts that you can easily put on or take off.
- **Comfortable Shoes:** Wear comfortable walking shoes suitable for both urban exploration and potential countryside trips.
- **Accessories:** Don't forget sunglasses, a hat or cap, and sunscreen for sunny days.

Clothing Recommendations

- **Casual Wear:** Opt for casual clothing, including jeans, shorts, skirts, and t-shirts, for exploring the city's attractions and streets.
- **Smart-Casual Options:** If you plan to dine in upscale restaurants or attend theater performances, consider packing some smart-casual outfits.
- **Dress in Layers:** As mentioned, layering is important. Bring a mix of short-sleeve and long-sleeve tops that can be combined for comfort.
- **Footwear:** Comfortable walking shoes are a must. Closed-toe shoes are recommended to protect your feet while walking on uneven surfaces.
- **Rainwear:** Given York's reputation for rain, pack a lightweight waterproof jacket or coat. Waterproof footwear or water-resistant shoes can also be helpful.
- **Evening Attire:** If you're planning to experience York's nightlife or dine in elegant restaurants, bring a few dressier options.

Specific Activities

- **Museum Visits:** Wear comfortable shoes for walking around museums, galleries, and historic sites. To transport necessities, think about packing a small bag.

- **Shopping:** Wear comfortable clothing and shoes for exploring boutiques, markets, and shopping districts.
- **Countryside Trips:** If you're planning day trips to the countryside or nearby attractions, consider packing outdoor-appropriate clothing, including sturdy footwear and weather-appropriate attire.
- **Theater or Performances:** If you're attending a theater show or performance, check the dress code. Smart-casual or semi-formal attire might be appropriate.

Practical Items

- **Backpack or Day Bag:** Bring a small backpack or crossbody bag to carry essentials, such as a water bottle, snacks, a map, and a camera.
- **Reusable Water Bottle:** Staying hydrated is important. To save money and lessen the amount of plastic waste, bring a reusable water bottle.
- **Electronics and Chargers:** Remember to bring chargers, your phone, and your camera. A power bank can be handy for keeping your devices charged.
- **Adapter:** If you're from a country with different electrical outlets, bring an adapter to charge your devices.

Local Customs

- **Respectful Attire:** While York is relatively relaxed in terms of dress code, it's recommended to dress respectfully when visiting religious sites or historic landmarks.

Remember that packing light is always a good idea. You can do laundry or buy items as needed during your trip. With the right mix of clothing and essentials, you'll be well-prepared to explore York comfortably and stylishly.

12.3 Health and Safety

Ensuring your health and safety is paramount during your trip to York. By following these guidelines, you can enjoy a stress-free and memorable visit:

- **Travel Insurance:** Before you embark on your journey, make sure you have travel insurance that covers medical expenses, trip cancellations, lost luggage, and other unexpected events.
- **Medications and Prescriptions:** If you take any prescription medications, ensure you have an adequate supply for the duration of your trip. Carry your medications in their original packaging and keep a copy of your prescriptions with you.

- **Emergency Contact Information:** Carry a list of emergency contact numbers, including local emergency services, your country's embassy or consulate, and your travel insurance provider.
- **Stay Hydrated:** Carry a reusable water bottle and drink plenty of fluids, especially if you're walking a lot or the weather is warm. Staying hydrated helps prevent fatigue and other health issues.
- **Sun Protection:** Wear sunscreen with a high SPF to protect your skin from the sun's UV rays. Use sunglasses and a hat to shield your eyes and face from direct sunlight.
- **Food and Water Safety:** While York has high food safety standards, it's a good practice to choose restaurants and food vendors that have good reviews and appear clean. Drink bottled water if you're concerned about tap water quality.
- **Know Your Limits:** Pay attention to your body and know your physical limits, especially if you're participating in outdoor activities or walking long distances.
- **Secure Your Belongings:** Secure your possessions to prevent theft or loss. Use a money belt or neck pouch to carry important documents, money, and cards.
- **Stay in Well-Lit Areas:** When exploring the city at night, stick to well-lit and busy areas to ensure your safety.

- **Local Emergency Services:** The emergency number in the UK is 999 for police, fire, ambulance, or other emergency services. Get to know the hospital or medical center that is closest to you.
- **Allergies and Dietary Restrictions:** If you have allergies or dietary restrictions, communicate them clearly to restaurant staff to ensure your meals are safe.
- **Plan:** Research the areas you'll be visiting and be aware of any safety concerns or local customs. Plan your routes, especially if you'll be walking around unfamiliar areas.
- **Trust Your Instincts:** Always put your safety first and trust your instincts if something doesn't feel right.

By staying vigilant, informed, and prepared, you'll be able to enjoy your trip to York with peace of mind. Remember that taking care of your health and safety is the foundation for a stress-free and enjoyable travel experience.

12.4 Local Laws and Customs

When visiting York, it's important to be aware of the local laws and customs to ensure a smooth and respectful experience. Here's an overview of some key aspects to consider:

- **Smoking Laws:** Smoking is prohibited in enclosed public spaces, including restaurants, pubs, and public transportation. If you must smoke, look for authorized smoking spots.
- **Alcohol Laws:** In the UK, 18 is the minimum age for drinking. You might be asked for identification when purchasing alcohol. It's illegal to drink alcohol in public places (except in areas specifically designated for that purpose).
- **Drug Laws:** Possession and use of illegal drugs are strictly prohibited in the UK. Offenses involving drugs can have harsh penalties.
- **Traffic Laws:** In the UK, vehicles drive on the left side of the road. Crosswalks are for pedestrians' use, and they should abide by traffic signs.
- **Public Behavior:** Public drunkenness, rowdy behavior, and disturbing the peace are not tolerated. Respect quiet zones, such as libraries and public transportation.
- **Respect for Historic Sites:** When visiting historic sites and religious landmarks, show respect by adhering to posted rules and guidelines. Avoid touching artifacts or structures unless explicitly allowed.
- **Photography and Privacy:** Always ask for permission before taking photos of people, especially in crowded areas. Some locations, such as museums and attractions, might have restrictions on photography. Look for signs or ask staff.

- **Waste Disposal:** Dispose of your trash properly in designated bins. Avoid littering in public spaces to maintain the city's cleanliness.
- **Noise Levels:** Be mindful of noise levels, especially in residential areas or places where people are trying to enjoy a quiet atmosphere.
- **Currency Transactions:** Counterfeit currency is a crime. Ensure that any cash you receive or use is genuine. When making purchases, verify the authenticity of banknotes.
- **Wildlife and Natural Areas:** Respect nature and wildlife in parks and natural areas. Avoid disturbing animals and follow any posted guidelines.
- **Local Respect:** Show respect for local customs, traditions, and cultural norms. This includes being polite and considerate to fellow residents.
- **Adapting to the Local Way:** Observe how locals behave and adapt to their customs. This will help you show respect for the local culture and blend in more naturally.

By familiarizing yourself with local laws and customs, you can ensure a respectful and enjoyable experience in York, while also contributing to the positive atmosphere of the city.

12.5 Avoiding Crowds

Avoiding crowds in York can enhance your experience by allowing you to explore the city's attractions and landmarks at a more leisurely pace. Here are some tips to help you make the most of your visit while minimizing the impact of crowds:

- **Choose Off-Peak Times:** Visit during the shoulder seasons of spring (March to May) or autumn (September to November) when the city is less crowded compared to the peak summer months. Weekends are typically busier than weekdays.
- **Early Mornings or Late Afternoons:** Arrive at popular attractions early in the morning or later in the afternoon when they are less likely to be crowded. This allows you to enjoy the sights without the rush of midday crowds.
- **Plan Around Peak Hours:** Attractions like York Minster and the Jorvik Viking Centre can get busy during mid-morning and mid-afternoon. Consider planning your visit during the opening or closing hours to avoid the busiest times.
- **Book Tickets in Advance:** Purchase tickets for popular attractions online in advance. This not only saves you time waiting in lines but also ensures you have a guaranteed entry time, reducing the risk of overcrowding.
- **Explore Hidden Gems:** While York's well-known attractions are popular for a reason, consider exploring lesser-known gems and quieter corners of the city. This might include

exploring local neighborhoods, small museums, or peaceful parks.
- **Take Guided Tours:** Joining guided tours can provide you with exclusive access and insights. Some tours offer early entry to attractions before they open to the general public, allowing you to enjoy them in a more intimate setting.
- **Avoid Peak Events:** Research major events and festivals taking place during your visit. While these events can be exciting, they might also attract larger crowds. If you prefer a quieter experience, plan around these dates.
- **Visit During Weekdays:** Weekdays are generally less crowded than weekends. If your schedule allows, plan your visit for Monday through Thursday to experience attractions with fewer tourists.
- **Plan Your Meals Strategically:** Restaurants and cafes can get busy during typical meal times. Consider having lunch slightly earlier or later than usual to avoid the peak lunchtime rush.
- **Be Flexible:** Keep in mind that even with careful planning, some attractions might experience unexpected crowds. Stay flexible and adjust your plans if necessary to avoid frustration.

By using these strategies, you can enjoy a more peaceful and immersive experience in York's historical and cultural treasures, allowing you to fully appreciate the city's unique charm and atmosphere.

12.6 Day Trips

York is not only a captivating city itself but also serves as a gateway to many charming destinations in the surrounding area. Here are some fantastic day trips and nearby attractions you can explore from York:

1. **Castle Howard:** Located about 15 miles from York, Castle Howard is a stunning stately home with beautiful gardens and impressive architecture. It's known for its role in film and television, including the TV series "Brideshead Revisited."
2. **Whitby:** About an hour's drive from York, Whitby is a picturesque coastal town known for its historic abbey, dramatic cliffs, and quaint fishing harbor. It's also famous for inspiring Bram Stoker's "Dracula."
3. **North York Moors National Park:** A short drive from York, this national park offers breathtaking landscapes, rolling hills, heather-covered moorland, and picturesque villages like Goathland (featured as Hogsmeade in the Harry Potter movies).
4. **Leeds:** Just about 25 miles away, Leeds is a vibrant city known for its shopping, dining, and cultural scene. Explore the Royal Armouries

Museum, museums, galleries, and shopping districts.
5. **Fountains Abbey and Studley Royal Water Garden:** A UNESCO World Heritage Site, this abbey ruins and stunning water garden are located around 30 minutes from York. Explore the historical ruins and the beautifully landscaped gardens.
6. **Harrogate:** Approximately 22 miles from York, Harrogate is known for its elegant architecture, the famous Betty's Tea Room, and the historic Turkish Baths. The town is also surrounded by lovely gardens.
7. **Rievaulx Abbey:** Situated in the North York Moors, Rievaulx Abbey is another striking historical site with well-preserved ruins set in a picturesque landscape.
8. **Scarborough:** This seaside town, about an hour from York, boasts beautiful sandy beaches, a medieval castle, and vibrant entertainment options, making it a popular destination for families.
9. **The Yorkshire Dales National Park:** A bit further out but worth the trip, the Yorkshire Dales offer stunning countryside, rolling hills, charming villages, and opportunities for outdoor activities like hiking and cycling.
10. **The Brontë Parsonage Museum in Haworth:** A journey to the heart of literary history, Haworth is where the Brontë sisters lived and wrote their famous novels. The

museum provides insight into their lives and works.
11. **National Railway Museum in York:** If you're a train enthusiast, you'll love the National Railway Museum right in York. It's home to an impressive collection of historic locomotives and carriages.
12. **York's Chocolate Story:** Discover York's chocolate heritage by visiting the York's Chocolate Story attraction, where you can learn about the city's rich history in chocolate production.

Whether you're drawn to historic sites, natural beauty, literary connections, or bustling cities, these day trips and nearby attractions offer a diverse range of experiences to complement your stay in York. Be sure to plan ahead, check opening hours, and consider transportation options to make the most of your exploration beyond the city limits.

BONUS

An Excellent 3-Day Itinerary

DAY 1

MORNING

Start your day by exploring the York Castle Museum, which offers a fascinating journey through the history of York. Through interactive exhibits and displays, find out more about the lives of those who resided and worked in the city.

AFTERNOON

Take a walk along the York City Walls, which are the most complete medieval city walls in England. Enjoy sweeping views of the city while learning about its history at the Henry VII Experience in Micklegate Bar, one of the gatehouses along the walls.

EVENING

The Shambles is a winding medieval street covered with timber-framed structures that are now used as stores, cafes, and restaurants. Eat a typical Yorkshire dinner at one of the neighborhood eateries, like The Star Inn the City.

BEDTIME: Find amazing hotels in York

DAY 2

MORNING

Immerse yourself in Viking history at the Jorvik Viking Centre, where you can explore a reconstructed Viking city and learn about the daily lives of its inhabitants. Afterward, visit the Merchant Adventurers' Hall, a medieval guildhall that offers a glimpse into York's trading past.

AFTERNOON

Visit York's Chocolate Story, a museum focusing on the origins of chocolate production in York, to satisfy your sweet taste. Learn how chocolate is made on a guided tour, then have a taste.

EVENING

Explore the Yorkshire Museum, which has a wide range of historical and natural history artifacts. Visit York Minster, one of Europe's most majestic cathedrals, to round off your evening, and if possible, take in a choral evensong service.

BEDTIME: Find amazing hotels in York

DAY 3

MORNING

Embark on a thrilling adventure at the York Dungeon, where actors and special effects bring to life the darker side of York's history. Afterward, climb Clifford's Tower, a medieval castle keep that offers panoramic views of the city.

AFTERNOON

Visit the National Railway Museum, which has a sizable collection of locomotives and railroad artifacts, to learn more about the intriguing world of railroads. Discover the history of British railroad development by exploring the antique carriages.

EVENING

Fairfax House, a gorgeously restored Georgian mansion that exemplifies the beauty and grandeur of living in the 18th century, invites you to travel back in time. Enjoy a candlelit tour and experience the opulence of the period.

BEDTIME: Find amazing hotels in York

Conclusion

As you close the final chapter of the "York Travel Guide 2025 and beyond," I hope that these pages have transported you to the enchanting streets, the hidden corners, and the rich history of this remarkable city. From the medieval marvels of the Shambles to the serene beauty of Rowntree Park, from the captivating stories of the past to the vibrant pulse of its present, York offers an experience that lingers long after the journey ends.

As you contemplate the adventures that await, consider the tales of the cat sculptures, the soothing embrace of the city walls, and the warm embrace of its friendly locals. Picture yourself strolling along the cobbled streets, discovering its treasured nooks, and savoring its culinary delights. The spirit of York is waiting to welcome you, to share its stories, and to create memories that will forever color your personal tapestry.

Before you set off on your voyage to York, remember that your voice matters. Just as these pages have guided you, your experience and insights can guide others. When you've explored the city's offerings, I encourage you to share your thoughts in a review, helping fellow travelers unlock the wonders that you've experienced.

May your journey to York be safe and seamless, filled with wonder and discovery. May you find new perspectives in the city's history and charm, and forge connections that transcend time. As you embark on this adventure, may your heart be light, your steps be joyful, and your memories be everlasting.

From these pages to the cobbled streets of York, I wish you the most incredible journey. Bon voyage!

Printed in Great Britain
by Amazon